THE JESUS LIBRARY

edited by Michael Green

THE SUPREMACY OF JESUS

Stephen Neill

HODDER AND STOUGHTON
LONDON SYDNEY AUCKLAND TORONTO

British Library Cataloguing in Publication Data

Neill, Stephen
The supremacy of Jesus.—(The
Jesus library)
1. Jesus Christ
I. Title II. Series
232 BT202

ISBN 0 340 27239 2

 Printed in Great Britain for Hodder and Stoughton Limited, Mill Road, Dunton Green, Sevenoaks, Kent by Richard Clay (The Chaucer Press) Ltd, Bungay, Suffolk

Hodder and Stoughton Editorial Office: 47 Bedford Square, London WC1B 3DP

CONTENTS

EDITOR'S PREFACE

I happen to know Stephen Neill well: and it is a privilege which I enormously treasure. We run jointly a Seminar for theological students in Oxford, and I, along with them, continually marvel at the wisdom, the breadth of learning, the grace and the shrewdness of this big-hearted Christian. His eyes twinkle with love and laughter: and often enough suffuse with tears as he reflects on what it cost the Lord to make himself known to sinners, and to rescue them.

All of these characteristics come across with great charm and compulsion in this astonishing book. He has, of course, magnificent credentials for writing it. He has already written extensively in the area: books such as *Christian Faith and Other Faiths, Colonialism and Christian Missions* come readily to mind, and he is engaged at present in writing the history of the Church in India in three volumes. He is a brilliant scholar of great simplicity and sophistication with much of his life spent in India as a missionary and bishop; much in the United States where he is a valued lecturer at leading universities; much in Germany where he was a professor in Hamburg; and no short time in Kenya where he was professor in the University of Nairobi. Nobody could say he was short of experience in the inter-faith debate!

This has become a central issue in Christian missiology these days. The shrinking of the world to a global village and the recrudescence of other faiths, often in a missionary spirit, to emphasise the value of their cultural heritance, has given a new look to Christianity. In many circles it is thought of as the white man's religion (although it is growing fastest among the brown and black populations of the world). In others it is thought of as a peculiarly Western phenomenon (though it is bursting out with great life in Asia, Africa and South America). But the man in the street, often abetted by syncretistic theologians, has gained the impression that most religions say very much the same, and that they are equally valid routes up the mountain to God.

Such theories will gain no support from this book. Instead, Bishop Neill shows with graciousness and candour the uniqueness and supremacy of Jesus over all contenders. There is nothing in this book which wants to take anything away from any other faith: it is not in Stephen Neill's character. Instead, there is ready appreciation for all that is good and true and lovely in other faiths. These things are rightly seen as partial aspects of the self-disclosure of God almighty who has revealed himself fully and decisively in Jesus Christ. The movement is from God to us, both in revelation and rescue.

I have never read a book on this subject with such breadth, insight and charm as this one. I am proud to include it in *The Jesus Library,* which is concentrating attention on various aspects of the life, death, resurrection and impact of Jesus which have either been obscured or forgotten in recent writings on the subject, and which have an important relevance to contemporary church life. It is a book with which those theologians of a different outlook will need to reckon, and at the same time one which the reader innocent of theology will be able to revel in. And there are not many books like that!

Michael Green

INTRODUCTION

The Central Point of History

The study of history cannot produce faith. But could historical and critical study of the Bible perhaps destroy faith?

'What is your beloved more than another beloved?' So the daughters of Jerusalem to the lady in the Song of Solomon. She answers in a splendid panegyric on the excellences of the one whom she loves, and ends with the words, 'This is my beloved and this is my friend, O daughters of Jerusalem' (S. of S. 5:9, 16).

The question is one that non-believers in nominally Christian countries, and adherents of other religions, have a right to put to Christians: 'What is your Christ more than any other Christ, that human beings are challenged to put their trust in him to the exclusion of any other Christ or Saviour?' Christianity is Christ. What lies at the centre of the discussion can be expressed succinctly in another question, 'What think ye of Christ?'

The Christian religion can be approached in a number of different ways. It is a rather elaborate system of doctrines, worked out by men of consummate ability over a number of centuries. It is a philosophy, with views on the nature of reality and on the destiny of man different from those put forward by other great thinkers through the ages. It is a system of ethics, contrasting so sharply with other systems as to constitute a constant and disturbing challenge. It expresses itself in a variety of forms of worship, in which resemblances which can be traced to the rites and practices of other faiths cannot obscure what is peculiar and original in the Christian way. All these different approaches, however, meet at one central point, and that point is Jesus, called the Christ.

Those who worked out the Christian doctrines were simply trying to express in words an inexpressible experience. With Jesus of Nazareth a new and immense force entered into human life; what was the origin of that force, and how are its operations to be understood and defined? The teachings of Jesus were not given in systematic form; but when they are put together and analysed, they are seen to amount to a total understanding of the universe, coherent and intelligible, though not without difficulties in detail. Christian ethics go back to the disturbing utterances of Jesus, in an attempt to do justice to their meaning without disrupting the whole of human life as it has been traditionally organised. When Christians end their prayers 'through Jesus Christ our Lord', this is no mere formula; the words express the Christian conviction that worship gives access to a new world, and that to this world Jesus holds the key.

If a number of reasonably well-educated persons were asked each to write down a short list of those men and women who in their opinion have influenced more than any others the whole of human life, it is probable that four names would appear on almost all the lists sent in–Gautama the Buddha; Jesus of Nazareth; the Prophet Muhammad; Karl Marx. It is notable that not one of the four was a ruler or conqueror. Alexander the Great, whose conquests set in motion the process which made Greek the common language of educated people from Hadrian's Wall to the foothills of the Hindu Kush, and Napoleon, whose *Code Napoléon* of laws survived his death and the disintegration of his conquests, might claim a place among the chosen few. Some poets and scientists might be included. But it is probable that the religious leaders would head the list. Of those whose names have been given, not one became a world figure until after his death; two of them lived in obscurity, little known beyond an intimate circle of friends and followers. Yet at least seventy-five per cent of the world's population live under the influence of the teachings of one or more of them; of the remainder, the majority would be classed as Hindus, adherents of the one great world religion which does not look back to a single historical founder.

The chosen four differed from one another in almost every conceivable way – in period, in country and language, in their manner of living and teaching. There is considerable diversity also in the ways by which we come to know them. Only one was a writer; the other three, as far as we know, wrote nothing down; for our knowledge of them we are dependent on what others wrote or said about them.

Karl Marx (1818-83) wrote endlessly. Scholars are still debating as to the meaning of what he wrote, and contrasting the earlier with the later Marx. His immense influence in the world today depends not so much on gifts of personality as on the cogency which many of those who have read his writings claim to have found in his arguments. His power lay in what he wrote rather than in what he was. In real life he seems to have been a rather disagreeable person, arrogant, always sure that he was in the right, and quarrelling remorselessly with those who ventured to disagree with him. But he did manage to retain throughout his life one devoted friend, Friedrich Engels.

Guatama the Buddha, as far as we can come to know him, shines out by contrast as a winning and charming person. Our difficulty in getting to know him is not that the materials are too few, but that they are too many. In the classic Pali canon, one-third of one of the three 'baskets' of which that canon is made up fills a thousand pages in the German translation. More than four hundred years had passed since the death of the Buddha before the canon reached its present elaborate form. Buddhist scholars tend to take an almost 'fundamentalist' view of these texts, treating as inspired every word that is ascribed to the great teacher. Western scholars take a rather more critical view; they hold that the canon records not so much the words of the Founder as the development of Buddhist doctrine and philosophy through the centuries, and that the historical evidence has to be extracted with difficulty from the mass of legendary incrustation by which it is in part concealed. Even in the great story of the death of the Buddha (the *Maha-parinibbana-Sutta*), in which we seem to be brought very near to the words and the spirit of the Master, there is much that the critical western reader will regard as legend rather than fact. But, for all the difficulties, what emerges from the record is a credible figure–always dignified, patient, not without humour, serene, surrounded by a group of faithful followers, and, like Jesus, with one beloved disciple, Ananda, who is with him at the time of his death. This is a teacher whom every sincere seeker of the truth must approach with respect, even with veneration, and with the desire to learn from him whatever of value he has to teach.

The story of Muhammad is a little like that of the Buddha. He wrote nothing; but from the Koran which he dictated, as he believed under the direct inspiration of God, much of the character of the man appears, and also a good deal of authentic history. We have to reckon also with three other sources. The first *Life* of the Prophet, that of Ibn Ishaq, is separated by no more than a hundred and fifty years from the events which it records. In addition, there are two immense collections, the *Sunna* and the *Hadith*, traditions which purport to record what the Prophet did or said on a great variety of occasions. Muslims do not regard these traditions as sharing in inspiration on the same level as the Koran, but attribute to them a considerable measure of authority. Western scholarship recognises some of these traditions as authentic but regards others as recording various stages in the development of Muslim thought and theology. Out of all these sources it is possible to construct a rather clear picture of a great man; less attractive, perhaps, than the Buddha, but a leader of men–vigorous, decisive, authoritarian, not always very scrupulous, but clear of purpose, and with an intense sense of knowing the will of God and being called to declare it. We shall do well to enquire into the nature of the experience of God by which the Prophet felt himself to be inspired, and which was his support in good days and in bad.

So we come to Jesus of Nazareth. Like Gautama and Muhammad he wrote nothing. But the records of his life and actions begin to appear very soon after his death. Not more than twenty years elapsed between that event and the writing of the earliest epistles. From secular historians we learn, as was to be expected, little or nothing of the Man of Nazareth. But many accounts of his life came to be written; as these came to be tested and sorted out, four, all written within at most a century of his death, were approved by the general consensus of the believers and found their way into the New Testament; the others survive only in fragments.

Why were some kept and the others rejected? The answer seems to be that Christians in the main stream of Christian belief would not let go their hold on history. Gnosticism, the first great rival of orthodox Christianity in the second century, was a system of ideas, of vivid pictures, of myth. Jesus does appear in the Gnostic writings, but the heavenly, mysterious figure there represented has little to do with the Carpenter of Nazareth. His manhood, in so far as it is recognised at all, is more of an appearance than a reality. The mind of the Church gradually rejected the mythical, and came to rest on those documents which deal unmistakably with the story of a man.

But what kind of history is it which comes before us in the four Gospels preserved in the New Testament? Clearly the Gospels are not annals, collections of disconnected facts strung together in mere chronological sequence. Luke at one point verges on the annalistic style (3:1-2) in an attempt to locate Jesus in the chronology of his age, but he has succeeded in puzzling us as much as he informs, and is not successful in giving the precision at which perhaps he aimed. Nor are the Gospels biographies in the ordinary sense of that term. They do not give clear evidence as to the year in which Jesus was born or as to the year in which he died. They tell us next to nothing of his early years, and concentrate on the brief period of his mission. Moreover, all these little books are written with a special purpose; they spring from a deep experience of faith, and are written to produce, or to strengthen, faith in the readers. So instruction is subordinated to challenge; the underlying question all the time is, 'What think ye of Christ?'

In consequence of this character of the documents, some scholars attach hardly any importance to the Gospels as history. What matters is that God has approached us in Jesus Christ, and that what happened long ago is brought near to us in the proclamation of the truth, in which the question of faith becomes 'existential', presented to us where we are and in our situation of the present day. So Rudolf Bultmann would reduce Jesus of Nazareth, in the brilliant phrase of the Italian scholar Giovanni Miegge, to the mathematical point which has position but no magnitude.

More modern scholarship has reacted against this extreme position. Bultmann is right in maintaining that tons of historical evidence will not produce so much as an ounce of faith. Such evidence might coerce assent, but that is a very different thing from faith. But, though history cannot produce faith, it can serve to undermine it. If it could be shown conclusively that Jesus of Nazareth never existed, the Gospels might continue to be good news, perhaps the best news possible for the perplexed and distracted human race. But Christian faith would become something very different from what it is. In the four Gospels, if they are taken seriously, we are dealing with a person who existed three-dimensionally in a part of the world's surface which we can exactly identify, during a period which we can determine within rather narrow limits. Confrontation with Jesus Christ cannot be separated from the question as to who and what he was.

Some years ago, a disciple of Rudolf Bultmann, Günther Bornkamm, was asked to write a book on Jesus of Nazareth.[1] By his own account, as he re-read the Gospels with a view to the writing of his book, he was astonished to find how much he could accept as historical. We now know a great deal about the world in which Jesus lived. The most sensational archaeo-

---

1. English translation, *Jesus of Nazareth* (London, 1960).

logical discovery of recent times, the so-called Dead Sea Scrolls, has thrown much less direct light on the New Testament than we had hoped; they have, however, helped to fill in the background of the Jewish religion as it was in the days of Jesus, and to make plain to us that it was more flexible and less rigid than we had been led to suppose. In all the Gospels there is an element of interpretation. Yet as we read them, we feel that we are in touch with a real person who moves on the stage of human history, one who like other great figures of history is at times perplexing in his acts and words, but who still remains identifiable and different from any other great religious teacher.

As we have nothing written by the hand of Jesus himself, we are dependent on the recollections of those who had known him, and on the writers who gathered together these recollections into continuous narrative. This does not mean that he is entirely lost in the mists of history. We may not be able to see him quite as clearly as we should like. But to see him, as we must, through the eyes of others does not mean that we cannot see him at all.

Every one of us lives in a variety of relationships, by which to a large extent our character and the course of our lives are determined. I have been a son to my parents, a brother to my brothers and sisters, an uncle to my nephews and nieces, a pupil to my teachers, a follower of those who have inspired me, a friend to my friends, a teacher to my pupils, a pastor to those who have been entrusted to my care, a citizen of the United Kingdom, a loyal member of a great college in Cambridge, a priest and bishop of the Anglican Communion – and so on, and so on; the list can be made almost endless. Happy the man or woman who stands in a great variety of relationships, and can knit them all together into the fabric of a unified personality.

Jesus, like the other great leaders of human thought, did not live a remote and cloistered life. The narratives make clear that at times he felt an urgent need to be alone. But the greater part of his time was spent in the company of other people. These people stood to him in a variety of relationships. Part of the sterling honesty of the Gospels is shown in the way in which they record the unkind things that were said of him by those to whom his methods and his message were too strange to be acceptable. The narratives also record the attitudes of friends, followers and disciples. All these saw him in different ways. If their testimonies do not always agree on every single point, this is nothing to be wondered at; it is a phenomenon with which we are familiar every day, in the varying estimates formed by people whom we know well of other people whom also we know well. But every careful and sympathetic observer will add something to our knowledge of others, both of those whom we have known, and of others whom we have not personally known.

It is not surprising that those who saw and heard Jesus formed different estimates of him, and that his contemporaries racked their brains to find the most satisfactory terms in which to express what they knew of him, and what they felt about him. Dr Vincent Taylor, in his book *The Names of Jesus* (1959), draws up a list (a complete list, I think) of all the names and titles used of Jesus in the New Testament. There are no less than fifty names and titles in the list. Some of them are poetical and allusive – 'the bright and morning star'; others are very ordinary and prosaic – 'the carpenter'. Some would be natural in the life of Israelites of his time – 'the son of David'; yet others imply profound problems of theology and philosophy – 'the Word'. Dr Taylor adds the interesting comment that, in all the centuries since the time of Jesus, believers have added only one title to those that are clearly present in the New Testament – the Redeemer.[2]

So Jesus is seen from many angles. To take a selection of these approaches, and of the names and titles by which they are designated, is a legitimate way of trying to get to know him. A prism will split up pure light into the seven colours of the rainbow; when the prism is withdrawn, pure light alone will

2. But note that the idea of 'redemption' is to be found in a number of contexts in the New Testament.

again be seen. When we have completed our study of Jesus through the prism of different titles, it may be hoped that the central figure will not have been lost in the variety of the approaches.

The underlying question which should be at all times in the mind of the student is this: 'What manner of man must he have been to whom all these titles have been given?' Of other great teachers we shall use the titles assigned to them by their followers and devotees, as most appropriate to each of them. We shall find that a number of the titles applied to other great leaders of human thought and religious experience – prophet, teacher, friend – are applied also to Jesus of Nazareth; this suggests that there are areas in which comparisons may legitimately be made between him and them. But the coalescence of so many titles on this one historic figure raises the question whether we may not here be in contact with something which is unique, and affords some grounds for the contention of Christians that their beloved is more than another beloved.

A Jew looks at the New Testament:

> *It should not be beyond the capabilities of an educated man to sit down and with a mind empty of prejudice read the account of Mark, Matthew and Luke as though for the first time.*
>
> Giza Vermes, *Jesus the Jew* (London, 1973), p. 19.

1

Human Nature: Reality and Caricature

Do we know what human nature really is? Or do we discover this only when we see Jesus?

It has often been noted that, through the centuries, the Church has found it easier to hold fast to the divinity of Christ than to his humanity. In much medieval piety Jesus appears as the 'Judge eternal throned in splendour', notably in Michelangelo's tremendous fresco of the Last Judgment in the Sistine Chapel in Rome. The son of man has been overshadowed by the Son of God. The incalculable debt we owe to the liberal theologians of the nineteenth century is the recovery of the Gospels as the story of a Man – the 'one mediator between God and men, the man Christ Jesus' (1 Tim. 2:5).

The most notable of the liberal lives of Jesus is that by the French scholar and sceptic Ernest Renan (1823-92), which appeared in 1863 (English translation 1864). Renan had many qualifications for the work he had undertaken. He was perfectly at home in that world of Semitic thought in which Jesus grew up; he had spent years in Palestine in the days before industrialisation had changed its traditional character. He wrote flawless French prose – his account of the death of Jesus is perhaps the most moving ever written outside the Gospels themselves. But Renan did not believe that the supernatural exists, and in consequence he included in his book everything about Jesus except those things that Christian believers regard as most significant. It is interesting to contrast with the *Life* by Renan the English *Life of Jesus* (1874) by Frederick William Farrar (1831-1903), the grandfather of Field Marshal Lord Montgomery. Learned, devout, eloquent, unquestioning, this book solves all problems by neatly evading them. It is not surprising that it was enthusiastically welcomed by conservatives as the final answer to unbelievers, and within a few years of the date of publication passed through a great many editions.[1]

So the Lives followed one after another, almost all of them catching something of the light of Jesus of Nazareth. But in 1906 Albert Schweitzer, who had read a great many of them, declared in his famous book on *The Quest of the Historical Jesus*[2] that it is impossible to write a life of Jesus: in the attempt we pull him out of the first century, in which he lived, into our nineteenth or twentieth century, and so miss the strangeness of what he really was. 'He comes to us', as Schweitzer writes on the last page of his book, 'as One unknown, without a name, as of old.'[3]

And yet not wholly unknown. We are faced by the phenomenon of the Christian movement. Many secular historians wish that this did not exist, and try to wish it away by pretending that it does not exist. But for all that it does exist – this strange movement, which, scorned by the elegant, persecuted by the malevolent, despised by philosophers, distorted by the uncritical, hated by the perverse, disregarded by the worldly, resented by the self-indulgent, ignored by the over-wise, has seemed again and again to die and yet has always managed to rise again from its own ashes, and in our century has presented us with the new phenomenon of a universal religion.[4] Starting as a movement for the most part among women and slaves, it has through the centuries exercised the brains of many among the ablest of mankind. It

1. The edition which lies on my table as I write is the seventeenth.
2. German, *Von Reimarus zu Wrede* (1906. Eng. trans. 1910).
3. Eng. trans., p. 401.
4. For verification, see the *World Christian Encyclopedia* (Oxford, 1981).

has won converts from every known religion upon earth, and has made itself at home in every area of culture. It has inspired great masterpieces of beauty in every field of art. It continues to grow and spread, and to assert itself in lands where a century ago the name of Jesus had not so much as been heard. It haunts our imagination.

What is behind it all? Movements do not simply arise out of themselves. They take advantage of propitious moments; movements which come into being at the wrong moment – too early or too late – do not ordinarily enjoy lasting success. But timeliness is a condition of success and not the cause of it. Behind the movements lies a man or woman whose genius was the spark that kindled into flame disparate elements of tinder.

History can be written either forwards or backwards. It is possible to start with the identifiable leader, to see how he seized opportunity, found the appointed sphere for the deployment of his gifts, and so set in motion something of the ultimate destiny of which he himself may have been hardly conscious. It is equally possible to start from the developed movement, to work backwards through various phases, to attempt to identify the kind of genius which must lie behind a movement of this kind, and then to check the inferences against the available historical evidence.

If every direct record of Adolf Hitler had been destroyed, it would still be possible to draw a convincing portrait of him by working backwards from what the Nazi movement became to its origins in a person. Circumstances were favourable. The gross inflation of 1923 – the German weapon against French aggression – had destroyed the savings and the hopes of the middle class. The myth that Germany had lost the First World War not through defeat in the field but through treachery at home, had kindled bitter resentments against those held responsible for the defeat. The mass unemployment resulting from the world economic crisis had left millions of people poor, hungry and disillusioned. One man saw his opportunity and struck. The endless scrolls of Hitler's table-talks, painfully recorded by his scribes, have pitilessly revealed the second-rateness of the man and the dreadful tedium endured by those who had to listen to his meanderings. It is strange that so gifted and cultured a people as the Germans so readily fell victim to his enchantments. But no one who has ever listened to his voice on the radio can doubt the almost hypnotic power he was able to exercise over crowds. The man had genius in turning dreams into realities.

I spent one of the most interesting evenings of my life on the banks of the Rhine in 1949 with three companions – a Dutchman, and two Germans, one of whom had risen high in the diplomatic service of his country. The diplomat began to reminisce: 'Mussolini was a much better man than Hitler,' he said. 'I knew Mussolini well, and of course I knew Hitler also. Our great mistake was in underestimating that man. You could lead me blindfold through ten rooms, and I would tell you without error in which of them the Führer was standing. There was an electric power that sparked out of him. If you have to deal with a man like that, there are only three choices before you – to give up politics and retire to your estates in the country, to sell yourself to him body and soul – or to bump him off.' If you are confronted with Jesus Christ, there are no estates in the country to which you can retire; the choices are not three, but two.

This element of challenge and potential strife runs all through the Gospels. Jesus himself gives dramatic expression to it: 'Do not think that I came to bring peace on earth; I have not come to bring peace, but a sword' (Matt. 10:34). Luke reads, 'I came to cast fire upon the earth', and then interprets it, correctly, 'not peace but rather division' (12:49-51). Some no doubt managed to remain in the wings, to be indifferent to Jesus and all that he stood for. But those who were prepared to take him seriously found inevitably that they had to stand on one side or the other – to serve or to destroy. A ship moving forward through the water cleaves it, and sets up a wave on either side. It cannot be otherwise. So it is with any forceful personality; the waves of attraction and repulsion will arise.

The death of Jesus has seemed to some so strange a conclusion to his career that they have interpreted it as a kind of trick by which God intervened to put things right that had gone seriously wrong. This is to disregard completely the evidence of the Gospels. The story could have had no other ending. Jesus being what he was, and men being what they are, the conflict was inescapable. Especially in Mark, the most dramatic of the Gospels, there is throughout a feeling of the shadows of destiny closing in, and of the working out of an inevitable tragedy. Goodness is always a threat to badness. If the bad will not yield to the good, they are almost bound in self-defence to attempt to destroy that which is seen to threaten what they are. Jesus, by what he was, proposed himself as a threat to a great diversity of human beings. In the last week of his life, all the streams of hostility flowed together into one, and, if he stood his ground, there could be no other end than death.

The Pharisees were very far from being wholly evil men. Paul bears generous testimony to them – 'they have a zeal for God, but it is not enlightened' (Rom. 10:2). They were the heirs of the Hasidim, the pious party among the Jews who stood for the purity of the law against compromise and dilution. Jewish writers of a later date have complained of the unfairness of the picture of them drawn in the Gospels, and to some extent they have a case. But the Pharisees were right in seeing that there was a fundamental opposition between their view of religion and that for which Jesus stood. Pharisaism held that a man can commend himself to God by scrupulous observance of the law; Jesus understood religion as total dependence on the free, generous and outgoing grace of God. Jesus's disregard of the strict Jewish rules of purity through his association with tax-gatherers and sinners, and his touching of lepers and other unclean persons, could not but be offensive to the upholders of the law as the final expression of the will of God.

The Sadducees were not basically irreligious, but their hold on religion was temperate, not to say tepid. They had managed to make an agreement with the Roman power under which they were able to exercise a considerable measure of authority. But their position was always precarious, dependent entirely on the goodwill of the Romans. In such a situation, the chief aim of the authorities is to see that no one rocks the boat. Of Jesus it was impossible to be sure that he would not rock the boat; and, therefore, it was better that he should die rather than that the whole nation should be imperilled. From his own point of view Caiaphas was perfectly right; he offers a perfect example of prudent political calculation (John 11:49-50).

Less is written in the Gospels about the Herods and the Herodians than about other groups, but we know a great deal about them from other sources. They were a gifted and intelligent family. Some of them had lived in Rome and were acquainted with members of the imperial house. They stood for a synthesis of Greek and Roman culture with that of the Jewish tradition. But their hold on the Jewish faith was tenuous. They were by origin not Jews but Idumaeans (Edomites); and, though they kept a palace in Jerusalem, they could hardly be regarded as convinced or practising Jews. The Greek culture in which they were interested was not characterised by the deep seriousness of the classical world, but was rather a showy and superficial adaptation of the heroic to the everyday. When confronted with the deadly seriousness of John the Baptist, Herod Antipas did not know what to make of him. His strange remark that in Jesus John the Baptist has come to life again is evidence of his perplexity. Jesus, when brought before him (Luke 23:6-12), can find nothing whatever to say to him – there is no common wavelength such as would make communication possible. Jesus is silent; Herod contemptuously dismisses him; no confrontation has taken place.

The perplexity of Pilate was a far more serious matter. To this day students of law go back to the Roman jurists to lay the foundations for an understanding of the basic principles of law. As governor, Pilate knew the difference between right and wrong, between justice and injustice. We know from other sources, as well as from the Gospels (Luke 13:1), that he was a harsh and unsympathetic ruler. To be procurator of Judaea was always an ungrateful task – the Romans did not know how to deal with the Jews, disliked them, and, like the satirist

Juvenal, wrote them off as a morose and ungracious people.[5] Pilate must have known that the charge brought against Jesus would not stand up to careful investigation, but for all that he gave him up to death, unaware that by so doing he was making himself, next to his victim, the most widely known character in the whole of human history.

If any mob in the world is confronted with Jesus and Barabbas, it is practically certain that it will choose Barabbas. We know nothing of Barabbas except that, at the excitable time of Passover, he had raised insurrection in the city and had committed murder. Presumably he was a member of one of those fanatically patriotic gangs, which were always ready to try the chance of an attack on the immensely superior power of Rome. Jesus had talked a great deal about the kingdom of God, but had done nothing to bring in that kingdom of David, of which so many Jews, eager for liberation from the yoke of Rome, were dreaming. When, if the report in St John's Gospel is to be accepted, some among the people came wanting to make him king, he solved the problem by simply running away and crossing the frontier into the neutral territory of Caesarea Philippi. Naturally the common people were enthusiastic for the man who had at least struck a blow for freedom, and were incensed with the one who had done nothing; the cry, 'Crucify him, crucify him', was the almost inevitable result.

So things worked themselves out to an end that could have been foreseen. The adversaries of Jesus had their way, and Jesus went on the way that they had planned for him.

The story in the Gospels is a beginning rather than an end.

Through all the centuries Jesus has been loved and hated. In modern times he has had a number of notable enemies. Friedrich Nietzsche (1844-1900) not merely declared that God is dead, but denounced Jesus as an impostor, whose creed exalted the servile qualities against the human virtues, and

---

5. *Satire XIV*, 96-106.

stood diametrically opposed to Nietzsche's plans for the emergence of the superman, towards whom humanity should be advancing. The barbed sarcasms of Lytton Strachey captured the fancy of many in the disillusioned generation after the First World War. In a two-volume biography Michael Holroyd has made plain what a large part hatred played in Strachey's make-up. He really hated Jesus Christ, whose moral standards he detested, and to whose claim on human loyalty and devotion he would not give a moment's consideration.

And yet Jesus Christ in his lifetime had a remarkable power of drawing men and women to himself. Confirmation of this understanding of his career has come from an unexpected source. The first serious attempt from the Marxist side to understand Jesus has come from the pen of a Czech Marxist, Milan Machoveč, under the title *A Marxist Looks at Jesus* (London, 1976), so much less appealing than the German title, *Jesus for Atheists* (Stuttgart, 1972). Machoveč will have nothing to do with the picture of the 'pale Galilean' popularised by Swinburne.[6] Whatever else we may think of him, Jesus was evidently a man of immense vigour and dynamism, with a remarkable power of drawing men and women to himself and holding their loyalty through good days and ill (p.81). It is good that this testimony comes from a writer who clearly has no prejudice in favour of the Christian view of Jesus.

But history shows that this view is correct. The importance of Peter's confession. 'Thou art the Christ', lies not so much in the fact that it was made, as in the fact that it was made when everything was going wrong. Jesus had done none of the things that were expected of the Messiah. He had made no direct messianic claim for himself. He seemed to accept all too easily the existence of Roman rule. He resolutely refused all political activity, and seemed too much absorbed in spiritual realities to be able to exercise any influence in practical affairs. And yet Peter was prepared to say, 'We accept you, though you do not

6. *Hymn to Proserpine* (*after the Proclamation in Rome of the Christian Faith*) (1866).

correspond to any ideas we may have formed as to what you ought to be'. He was beginning to understand, albeit at that time very dimly, that Jesus creates his own dimension, and will not allow himself to be fitted into any framework that we have prepared for him. When Peter affirmed that, if need be, he was prepared to die with Jesus, the others all said the same. The record tells us plainly, with its usual concern to be true rather than pleasing, that over-confidence betrayed them and that they were not as brave as they supposed. But Jesus had said that faith as a grain of mustard-seed would suffice. They had found a leader whom they could trust, and they would not let him go. Events were to show that faith even as a grain of mustard-seed was enough, and would enable them both to stand the shock of his death and also to carry forward his work in the world.

What is this strange gift of attraction that some men and women have and others have not? It is hard to define, yet without it men and women do not become leaders. Much nonsense is talked these days about leadership, and not least in church circles. Many so-called leadership training courses might succeed in producing reasonably efficient business executives, but no more. The gifts of leadership can be developed by self-discipline, attention to opportunity, and by a certain recklessness, but only if the initial qualities of idealism, courage and firmness in decision are present. These gifts can be dangerous, since they can be turned to bad uses as well as to good ones. The qualities of leadership were certainly present in that strange fanatic John Brown (1800-59), gaunt, uncouth, obsessed by the idea that he had a divine call for the freeing of the slaves; he was able to persuade two of his own sons, who knew him better than anyone else, and a number of other apparently reasonable people, to accompany him on the enterprise, hopeless from the start, of Harper's Ferry (16 October 1859). They hanged John Brown, but he left a name and a legend behind him.

Clearly Jesus had this attractive power in an unusual degree. It proved itself no less in relation to women than to men.

Part of the reason for this may be that he unites in himself qualities which are usually held in separation, and some of which are more often seen in women than in men. He combines unhesitating authority with a total lack of self-assertion; courage in the face of danger with almost feminine tenderness in affection; the harshest judgment on the self-satisfied and the complacent, with winning kindness to sinners and those who are out of the way.

Christians have been inclined to claim that in him we see the universal man. Many critics have objected to this Christian view. For example, David Friedrich Strauss, whose *Life of Christ* (1836) still stands as a landmark in the critical study of the New Testament, wrote in Hegelian phrase that, 'the Idea loves not to pour all its fulness into one example, in jealousy towards all the rest'.[7] But this utterance seems to rest on a misunderstanding. In point of fact the individual is the universal. The more sharply distinguished the individual is from all his fellows, the more significant he becomes for them all. This is well known to the great dramatists. Those lesser writers who have dealt in types have produced nothing better than lay figures, who cease to be interesting as soon as we have seen through them. Shakespeare has a unique faculty of making even his minor characters living persons whom we can recognise from the few lines in which he has drawn them, just as Rembrandt can picture for us a whole life-career in the face of one old man. Lady Macbeth speaks only a hundred and sixty lines in the play which she shares with her husband, but she is both herself and the whole race of perplexed, unhappy women. We have all been Hamlet in his indecisions and uncertainties; yet we can never be sure that we have penetrated all the depths of his being.

More than any other Jesus is both himself, an individual unlike any other individual in human history, and also the

7. The comment of the Scottish theologian H.R. Mackintosh on 'this strange misconception' is that 'the love of God is concentrated in Jesus only that it may fill the world' (*The Person of Jesus Christ*, p.438).

whole human race. When we think that we have caught him and pinned him down, he slips between our fingers, and beckons us onward from a distant point of vantage. This is why no one has ever succeeded in writing a fully satisfactory life of him.

Perhaps we shall express the matter better if we say that Jesus gives us a clear answer to the question of what it really means to be a human being.

Great advances have been made in the twentieth century in psychology, the study of human nature in its heights and in its depths. We have begun to understand the mysterious world of the sub-conscious and the unconscious. Part of the difficulty of the study arises from the uncertainty in the minds of students and professors of the art as to the nature of the *psyche*, indeed as to whether there is any such reality as the *psyche* at all. Much of the time of the psychiatrist is spent in the attempt at healing, and for this he has to deal mainly with the abnormal, or rather with those in whom abnormality has reached a point at which it proves harmful to the victim and possibly dangerous to others. It is hard for him to fix on any standard of normality, or even to convince himself that there could be any such thing.

The Greeks believed that they could work out standards to determine the perfection of the human form and of male and female beauty. Their success is evident in such masterpieces as the Hermes of Praxiteles and the Venus of Milo. The Renaissance took up the quest again, as soon as the medieval prejudice against the unveiling of the human form had been overcome. Michelangelo's David is perhaps the most splendid expression of the Renaissance understanding of what it really means to be a man.

Is it conceivable that in Jesus Christ we can see what it means to be fully and completely human?

It is fairly easy to make from the records a list of human characteristics that are evident in him. Clearly there was great intellectual ability; though he was not technically well-educated, he could speak profoundly on all the great problems that encircle humanity. His handling of the Old Testament shows an imaginative grasp of words and themes. His poems reveal sensitivity in relation to nature, and also in the use of words. The brilliance of his dialectic in answering questions shows a quick and ready mind. Humour is not stressed; that it was there cannot be doubted by anyone who has watched in imagination a Pharisee swallowing a camel. He can overhear the whisper in the crowd, and sympathise with the perplexity of the father of the epileptic boy, who finds it difficult to believe (Mark 9:21-23). These gifts do not exist in isolation, still less in conflict with one another. All are at all times at his disposal. All work together rhythmically and harmoniously towards one central purpose.

There are considerable differences between individuals in intellectual ability. But these are probably less than is often supposed; the differences may be not so much innate as caused by differences of environment and opportunity. Similarly there are great differences of will-power. To some extent these may be due to the genes – some people are naturally more forceful than others. But to a large extent they may be due to the divided will, of which we are all conscious. There is one will which says 'Yes' and another which says 'No'. One will says, 'Go ahead, in spite of some difficulties or even dangers.' The negative will says, 'The dangers are so great that it is better to stay where you are.' The result of this inner dialogue is hesitation and indecision. If the arguments are evenly balanced, the result may be the perplexity of the donkey between two equidistant carrots – the will seems paralysed and any decisive action becomes impossible. If the will were always clearly directed to one aim, dynamic action would at all times be possible.

In some human beings decisiveness is seen in a very high degree indeed. Of the first Napoleon, Lord Rosebery wrote in his discerning work *Napoleon, the last Phase* (1900, p.252), that he has permanently enlarged our understanding of what it is possible for a human being to achieve. The result was not an attractive personality. After one set-to with him, the polished and cynical Talleyrand was heard to remark, 'How regrettable that so great a man should be so ill-bred.' The one central aim of Napoleon was the exaltation of Napoleon. To this he bent his very considerable intellectual gifts, his ruthlessness, his military skills, his gift of rapid decision, his power to dominate the wills of other men. He came near to dominating the world; but the end of it all was St Helena.

Jesus exhibited a similar dynamic power on a higher and a nobler level. The one aim on which all his gifts were concentrated was the proclamation and the establishment of the Kingdom of God. In this there was no room for personal ambition or self-concern. It was this that gave him his mastery in every situation; even in the desolation of the cross he rules as Lord of men and Lord of history.

Bishop John Robinson in *Honest to God* gives to one chapter the title 'The Man for Others'. This is as good a summary as can be given of the nature of the life and ministry of Jesus. This self-renunciation is not to be understood as hatred of self – this, where it exists, is always a neurotic symptom. It is simply recognition of the truth that the way to self-fulfilment is not through self-assertion but through self-denial. This is perfectly in accord with accurate psychological observation. The self-centred individual is always under strain and usually unhappy. 'What do others think of me? Am I where I ought to be? Am I making full use of my powers? Are my powers failing? Do I do as well as I used to do, and as I need to do, if I am to get to the top of the tree?' The self which is so concerned for the welfare of others that it has no time for concern about the self is free, untrammelled, joyful, and often far more effective than the calculating self so sorely concerned about its own advancement.

Fortunately the life for others is not found exclusively among Christians. Altruism of the purest and most generous kind is found among people of other faiths and of no faith. But it is so supremely seen in Jesus of Nazareth that Christians feel justified in inviting others to look at him. It was this attitude, unvaried through his whole life, as far as we know it, which enabled him at the end to say, 'Be of good cheer. I have overcome the world' (John 16:33). The Christian ventures to hope that by trying to follow him, the servant may attain to some measure of the serenity which so clearly radiates from the Master.

> *Jesus 'doctrine'... set the world on fire not because of the obvious superiority of his theoretical programme, but rather because he himself was at one with the programme, because he himself was the attraction. They saw in him a man who already belonged to this coming Kingdom of God; they saw what it meant to be 'full of grace', what it meant to be not only a preacher but himself the product of his preaching, a child of the future age to the marrow of his bones.*
>
> M. Machoveč, *A Marxist Looks at Jesus*, pp.82-3, 90.

2

Moses and Law: Jesus and Liberation

We are not under law but under grace – the grace of our Lord Jesus Christ. But does this mean that we can do whatever we like?

The great Augustine once wrote, '*Ama et fac quod vis*' – love and do whatever you wish. When he wrote this, was he stringing together words without meaning? Or was he expressing a purely personal preference? Or was he making a profound statement about the nature of the universe? Christians are committed to the third view – that all ethical statements are also metaphysical statements – that is, that they are related to a total view of the nature of the universe in which it is our fate to dwell.

This has been for a number of years a subject of considerable debate among philosophers.

Some would not agree that ethical statements, i.e. statements involving the idea of moral obligation or responsibility, can have relevance to ultimate reality. But, in so doing, they are themselves making a metaphysical statement, in denying that this universe is such that statements involving the idea of moral issues, moral obligations, or moral responsibilities can be made about ultimate reality as we know it. Such an affirmation should not be accepted without careful scrutiny of the evidence on which it is based.

Others are inclined to the view that ethical statements, i.e. those that relate to such ideas as 'good' or 'bad', are meaningless, except in so far as they may be used to give expression to a personal preference. The words used taken separately may have significance, but taken together in a sentence they can have no meaning, as being unrelated to any existent, of which the existence is observable or verifiable.

The objection, when put forward by thoughtful critics, has considerable weight. The meaning of 'meaning' is a philosophical problem of great significance, to which no more than allusion can be made. The critics have drawn the attention of Christians to the importance of paying exact attention to the meaning of words, such as 'good' and 'bad' which they habitually use, and to be sure (as the critic is confident that they cannot be) that sentences, affirmations, judgments have such meaning as will commend itself to any thoughtful man.

It is much less easy than unskilled speakers and writers imagine to compose even a single sentence of which the meaning and relevance is absolutely clear. One or two examples may be given of the way in which things may go wrong.

It is quite easy to put together disconnected words, each of which in separation has a meaning but which together make no conceivable sense. If I write down at random the words 'pigeons cloud directionally imitative', this might be supposed to be some mysterious code, or some expert Freudian might deduce from it some hidden secret of my emotional processes. But in point of fact I wrote down the words at random, and, if I had any intention, it was simply that of excluding as far as I could the possibility of any recognisable meaning.

The sentence, 'All zebras have five legs', has a quite clear and definite meaning; but it makes no sense since it contains a semantic contradiction, inasmuch as by dictionary definition a zebra is a living creature which has four legs; there could be very rare five-legged aberrations, but the sentence as it stands is insignificant.

The sentence, 'Centaurs are only rarely found in Yorkshire', makes grammatical sense, but is meaningless as having no reference to anything. A centaur is a creature of which the legs and body are those of a horse, but the torso and the head are those of a human being. In this universe, such creatures do not exist outside the world of romantic imagination, and therefore there are none to be found in Yorkshire or anywhere else; there may be other universes in which such creatures are to be found; in those the sentence might make sense.

'Two and two make five' has a perfectly clear grammatical sense, but it means nothing because it is based on a miscalculation. In the ordinary realms of arithmetic, two and two can make four and nothing else; though the sentence could be given a metaphorical sense, if used of an adventurous thinker, of the kind that makes two and two equal five; but the exaggerations of poetry must not be construed as though they were plain prose.

The term 'meaningless' may therefore be correct in certain connotations, but a variety of nuances can be detected in the way in which it can be used, and it is important to be sure in each case of the variation with which we are dealing.

The expression, 'thou shalt not kill', has a perfectly clear and defined meaning, both in the separate words, and in the sentence as a whole. To kill is to bring life, an identifiable reality, to an end in such a way that the living is replaced by the un-living. The reality is, in fact, only emphasised by the wit of A.H. Clough's paraphrase:

> Thou shalt not kill; but need'st not strive
> Officiously to keep alive.

It is not, as some would maintain, semi-jussive – 'Please do not kill me.'

It is not, as others would hold, a mere statement of feeling, of an emotional attitude: 'On the whole I would prefer that you should not kill me, or others.'

It is an affirmation of the nature of the universe in which we live, that is, it is a metaphysical statement. If an expanded version is desired, it would run something like this: 'In this universe, one of the most valuable things we have encountered is human life and personality; therefore no individual may take on himself the responsibility for bringing any human life to an end, except in the special case of taking life in self-defence, or to save the life of others who are threatened with extinction.' Now it is possible that those who hold this view are mistaken. There may be in the universe no recognisable scale of values such as would make it possible to maintain that human life is in itself valuable. It might be possible to recognise in the universe no such order as would justify the making of any general statements about it. But that does not make the sentence, 'Thou shalt not kill', meaningless. The argument is not about words and phrases but about the nature of things, the nature of reality, and in particular, the nature of human beings in society.

The science of ethics deals with human beings in a variety of relationships.

The physical scientist endeavours to ascertain the nature of the physical universe, and of those continuities and regularities which are sometimes known by the not very accurate term 'laws of nature'. The enucleation of these principles has proved a difficult task, but a good deal of progress has been made. Few people today would deny that the heliocentric understanding of the solar system is truer, in that it holds together in readily intelligible form more actual and accurate observations than the old Ptolemaic or geocentric system. No one now believes in phlogiston, though the idea of phlogiston served many useful purposes, until it was discovered that the gas called oxygen is a constituent part of both air and water.[1] Much of the progress of science has taken place through the tireless collection and classification of details.

But some sudden leaps forward have come about just because some inspired person asked an obvious question which no one had ever asked before. Dr. T.S. Kuhn has written a

---

1. Phlogiston, a mysterious substance which, though not fire itself, is the material of fire. The phenomenon of oxidation had been observed long before the identification of oxygen.

fascinating book under the title *The Structure of Scientific Revolutions.*[2] The list of revolutionaries would include Copernicus, Galileo, Newton, Lavoisier, Einstein, Planck, Dirac, Heisenberg and others. And most conveniently, on the day before these pages were written, *The New York Times*[3] published an article on 'The Art of Teaching Science' by Dr Lewis Thomas, the theme of which is that science should be taught today not in terms of established results, but in terms of mystery: 'We do not understand much of anything, from the episode we rather dismissively (and, I think, defensively) choose to call the "big bang" all the way down to the particles in the atoms of a bacterial cell. We have a wilderness of mystery to make our way through in the centuries ahead.'

When life appears, things become increasingly more complex than in the realm of what we call the lifeless, the material. We now know a great deal more than we did about the way in which life works, but we do not seem to be much nearer knowing what life actually is. It is possible that one day scientists may succeed in producing a living thing out of the non-living in the laboratory. If I am asked how this would affect my faith, I would answer simply, 'Not at all.' This would not really bring us much nearer to knowing how life first appeared on this planet, when there were no scientists, no laboratories or test-tubes to produce it.

When life develops into human self-consciousness, the difficulties once again become enormously greater. How in the world am I to understand this vast mass of intelligent beings, each of whom operates in wholly unpredictable curves and gyrations, and who in their freedom, limited though that may be, so easily break through any classification we try to impose upon them? Are there any rules, and if so where are they to be found?

We have said that ethical studies deal with men in relationships. There is first man's relationship to his environ-

---

2. University of Chicago Press, 6th impression, 1974.
3. 14 May 1982.

ment – rocks and stones and water, plants and living creatures. In recent years, we have been brought up sharply to face our responsibility to the world that surrounds us. We are beginning to recognise the horrible cruelty of men in destroying interesting and beautiful species, and the impoverishment we have inflicted on ourselves by the reckless destruction of woods and forests. Then there is man's relationship to himself. Research has shown how much physical illness is caused by, or related to, inner disharmony – man does not know how to live at peace with himself; this is perhaps why we find it so difficult to live at peace with other selves. Then there is the mutual relationships of human beings in society. This, the most complicated of all, is the sphere of ethical research, and of moral understanding. But the Christian holds that human existence is not three-dimensional but four-dimensional. Down certainly to the world around; inwards to ourselves; outwards to our human world; but it does not become truly human until it includes the upward direction to that eternal reality to which Christians and others give the name God.

All societies have rules by which conduct is directed and controlled, and which are enforced by a variety of sanctions. In the vast majority of cases, these are unwritten but are preserved in the memory of the elders, and passed on to the coming generation in those rites of passage which play an essential part in the transition from puberty to manhood. Whence these rules came no one knows for certain; they may be attributed to some remote ancestor of the peoples, more often they are of nameless origin. Even among the simplest peoples these rules are highly complex, unsystematic and not held together by any clear principles, yet still binding on all members of the community. But just as science progresses through the hunches that come to specially gifted people, so understanding of man in society and of the principles that should govern his life, is in many cases advanced by the insights of the gifted thinker or lawgiver who brings order out of chaos and thinks through to the principles on which the good ordering of society can be based. *Natura simplex est* was a saying of the great Sir Isaac Newton.

Among the Greeks, Aristotle thought deeply about ethics, and wrote more than once on the subject, his best-known work being the *Nicomachean Ethics*. As is to be expected of so great a thinker, the work is full of insights of lasting value. Aristotle establishes the principle of 'nothing in excess'; virtue will be found in the golden mean. Courage is to be found at the median point between timorousness and recklessness; the right use of possessions on the middle line between parsimony and extravagance. The weakness of these ethics is that the principles are worked out for free man in a society in which the majority were slaves; the ideal is that of the magnanimous or high-spirited man, one who can hardly be expected to practise these virtues except in an atmosphere of freedom.

Almost contemporary with Aristotle was Confucius, whose *Analects* have exercised an influence on human society as profound as that of any great monument of thought. China has been Confucian for more than two thousand years; it seems likely that, as the rough influence of Mao Tse-tung wanes, the aristocratic Confucian influence may rise again to the surface of Chinese life, though it is unlikely that China will ever go back to what it was before the revolution. But here once again we are dealing with an aristocratic code; Confucius is laying down the code of conduct for a cultivated man in a polite and sophisticated society; he hardly takes account of the level on which the majority of men in society live.

Neither Aristotle nor Confucius presents ethics in relation to any formal religion. Worship of the gods in Athens was a matter of decent conformity rather than of conviction. The attitude of Confucius towards spirits is that the wise man will treat them with respect, but will have as little to do with them as possible. Scholars will debate to the end of time the question whether Confucianism should be regarded as a religion or no. In Israel, and in the religions which have grown out of origins in Judaism, ethics and religion are inseparable aspects of one comprehensive understanding of the life of human beings, and of the nature of the universe in which we are called to live.

The Jews looked back to Moses as the supreme lawgiver by

whom the pattern of the life of the nation was determined once for all. As often happens, many stories have gathered about the head of this great figure, who combined in himself the office of prophet, priest and lawgiver. Scholars are not yet agreed as to the extent to which these stories can be accepted as historical in the narrow sense of the term. But, if Moses had never existed, it would have been necessary to invent him. A mob of slaves, after a period of Bedouin wandering in the wilderness, is formed into the core of a nation, which has survived for more than three thousand years. How did this come about?

The Hebrew youth, who grew up as the son of Pharaoh's daughter, who was condemned to many years of exile in the desert and was then called to bring his people out of Egypt with signs and wonders and to lead them through the wilderness to the promised land, presents just the figure that is needed to fill a gap in history. Israel looked back to Moses as the man with whom God spoke as a man speaks with his friend, whose heart was almost broken by the perversity of the gang of freed slaves it was his lot to command, who received from the very hand of God the principles of the royal law by which Israel was constituted a nation.

It was, I think, G.K. Chesterton, who noted that, if a rather elaborate key was picked up somewhere in the desert and was later found to fit exactly a certain lock, there would be good reason to suppose that that key was made to fit that lock. If a set of precepts laid down three thousand years ago for a horde of Bedouin is found to be of such universal validity that to this day it can be read in the Christian liturgy, and since the time of Luther has been used in a great many churches as part of the instruction of candidates for baptism or confirmation, there is reason to suppose that the ten commandments are something more than a set of random precepts laid down a long time ago for a society that no longer exists. Laws such as these are not edicts arbitrarily laid down by an authority which exacts obedience from reluctant subjects. The ten commandments are, in point of fact, a brilliant analysis of the minimum conditions on which a society, a people, a nation, can live a sober, righteous and civilised life.

Physicists have shown us that the physical universe is made in one particular way and not in any other particular way. The genius such as Moses, who has a special understanding of the nature of man, tells us that the world of man in society is made in one particular way and not in any other particular way. It is possible for man to work havoc on the world of nature, and it is possible for man to work havoc on the life of man in society; but this can be done in each case only by ignoring or flouting the principles on which each has been constituted.

The ten commandments are not a random set of ethical rules. They lay down the principles for a people which wishes to be a people of God. God, who has delivered them out of Egypt, says to them, 'I am a particular kind of God; if you want to be my people, you must be a particular kind of people – and these are the rules.' So it is no accident that the first three commandments deal with the relationship between God and man. God's claim is exclusive; any kind of polytheism is excluded. The vast and complex idolatry of Egypt and Assyria is not to be so much as mentioned by a people whose God is known as the creator of heaven and earth. Man must always approach God in the spirit of reverence and adoration, as the 'One who is' – 'I am that I am' (Exod. 3:14).

Only then do we come to the rules for human beings living with human beings. Here it is to be noted that the seven commandments which follow are not a handbook of individual ethics. The individual is not disregarded, but throughout the Old Testament God is seen as dealing primarily with a people – a people that, for all its aberrations, does desire to be the people of God.

When man and beast live and work together, both man and beast stand in need of rest. Experience shows that one day's rest in seven is the minimum requirement for optimum efficiency. In any organised community, there must be authority. Authority is vested primarily in the elders, the 'fathers and mothers', who in all simpler societies are the guardians of the traditions, and are to be respected for the accumulated riches of wisdom which they are to use for the good of the community. No man or woman should need to go about armed; the blood feud, which was in full force in parts of Arabia within living memory, is to be a thing of the past.[4] In such a community the family is immensely important; the man or woman who looks outside the wedding ring threatens the stability of the community as a whole. No society can exist without a certain amount of private property. Three methods only of acquiring property are sanctioned as legitimate – as payment for services rendered, as free gift, as fair exchange. Anything outside of these is robbery, an offence against the general well-being. The reputation of every member of the community should be safe in the hands of the other members; if there are offences, they can be dealt with openly, but not by the craft and underhandedness of the whisperer, the false accuser. If there is strife within the community, it can in a great many cases be traced back to jealousy; contentment with what you have, not necessarily excluding a desire to better yourself by legitimate means, is the high road to happiness and peace.

If all the inhabitants of Great Britain were to take this simple code in its most literal sense and to live by it, it would be possible to make enormous reductions in government spending. When I was a boy in the country, we never thought of locking our front door at night; why should one? That today we have to lock everything up so carefully is evidence that we have not yet caught up with Moses in the wilderness.

The greatest breakthrough into an understanding of this world of men and of the way in which it is constituted came with Jesus of Nazareth. Moses dealt in the main with the way in which relationships are expressed in actions; Jesus looks beyond these to the heart – to thoughts and attitudes. Intention cannot be wholly excluded from the consideration of the law courts; an entirely accidental infliction of damage is not

---

4. For fascinating tales of the blood-feud and its elimination, see H. Ingrams, *Arabia and the Isles* (1942).

criminal; this is recognised even by the law of Moses. Jesus goes further. To be angry with your brother brings you under the judgment of God. Not unnaturally, many of the Greek manuscripts of the New Testament soften this down by adding 'without cause'.

Very few of the laws laid down by Jesus Christ are time, place or situation conditioned. He was, of course, a Jew and spoke in the language of his time. When he wished to see a coin, it was naturally for the Roman denarius that he called. This had on it the head of the emperor, and therefore, though the Jews used it in ordinary commercial transactions, it could not be admitted into the temple. Such use of local custom was natural, and does not in the least qualify the universal relevance of the lesson Jesus wishes to teach – of limited obligation to the human authority, and unlimited obligation to the divine. He gives few direct orders. Of those that he does give, hardly a single one is conditioned by any particular limitations of time and space. In this he differs markedly from those other great lawgivers, Moses and Muhammad.

Beyond the simple affirmations of the ten commandments, the law of Moses gradually expanded into a vast, rambling, and not wholly consistent body of regulations. These fall into three distinct classes. There are general principles revealing the nature of the God of justice. There are rules of hygiene, intended to keep clean and healthy an encampment of nomads in the wilderness (e.g. Deut. 23:9-14). It is interesting that these have been preserved in a much later collection of laws, though in detail they are not applicable to city life. Thirdly, there are many particular regulations which begin with the formula: 'if a man ...', 'when a man ...' These are gradually built up into a handy code of procedure. It is, in most cases, possible to go behind the detail to the principle involved, so much so that the chapters in Deuteronomy, in which many of these regulations are set forth, have been called by the general term the 'law of compassion'. The Rabbis gradually expanded these biblical rules into a mass of prescriptions and prohibitions, to cover every conceivable situation and giving detailed instructions on almost anything that may occur in daily life, so much so that a book of Jewish law compiled for use at the present time fills many hundreds of pages.

Muhammad was concerned to knit together the believers in his message into a recognisable and law-abiding community. The creed he handed over to them was the shortest and simplest in the world; but as a moral reformer, he thought it wise to legislate, as he believed entirely under divine inspiration, for many situations that arise in the course of the organisation of the community. He was a man of his own time; inevitably a number of the rules that he laid down reflect the society of Arabia in the seventh century and are less applicable to the societies which developed in other countries on different lines.

It is laid down in the Koran that a man may have four wives, and an unspecified number of relationships outside marriage. No doubt this was a great improvement on the promiscuity with which Muhammad had to contend in the Arabia of his day; it has, however, proved an embarrassment in a world in which monogamy is the generally accepted form of the marriage relationship. During the fast of Ramadhan, the believer is expected to refrain from eating or drinking from dawn till sunset; this is not too grievous a discipline in lands near the equator; it becomes hard to bear in countries in which in June or July daylight may last for sixteen hours.[5] In a number of Muslim countries, the question has been raised whether, in an industrialised society, a man can be expected to do a full day's work under the exacting conditions of a factory, if he has had nothing to eat since before sunrise. Can the spirit of the fast be kept without strict adherence to the letter? The Muslim fundamentalist will at once answer that to make a distinction between letter and spirit is itself an evidence of unbelief; the Muslim commands may be exacting, but they are not beyond the powers of a man to obey – if he has the will to obey.

---

5. In the year 1982 Ramadhan did actually occur in June and July.

In addition to what can be directly derived from the Koran, the faithful Muslim is faced by an immense number of detailed rules, descending to the minutiae of personal and sexual hygiene. To know all of these demands effort; to keep all the rules means constant watchfulness. The Christian may be thankful that he is spared this burden of legality – until he observes that the simplicity of the commands of Jesus is complemented by their extreme exigency. To the complaint of legalism, the Muslim has his answer ready: Muhammad was the practical reformer; he knew the limits of human capacity, and did not pitch his demands higher than can be attained by the men and women of good will, whose purpose is set on obedience to the will of God. But the counter-question is this: Is it better to have a rather low ethical ideal to which it is possible to attain without extraordinarily severe efforts, or to have an ideal so high that we shall never be able to scale its summits, but shall be stimulated to press on, ever a little nearer to the unattainable? The Christian is in no doubt as to the answer that he will give to this question.

Aristotle, Confucius, Moses, Muhammad – all of these pondered the nature of man in society, and each made a notable contribution to understanding. It has, however, been suggested earlier in this chapter that the mind of Jesus is more penetrating, and his understanding of human society more precise, than that of any of these others. But, as in the case of Moses, the vision of Jesus does not hang in the air; it is related to a singularly clear vision of who and what God is; ethics are not separated from religion, but are simply the expression, in one sphere, of faith in God, and can be summed up as the doing of God's will. One of the noblest of the utterances of Plato is that the best destiny for man is to be made as much like God as possible,[6] a sentiment which every Christian can adopt without qualification. The Epistle to the Hebrews applies to Jesus the words of the Psalmist: 'I come to do thy will, O my God.' This is not servile submission to an arbitrary tyrant, but joyful

6. *Theaetetus*, 176 b.

acceptance of that supreme relationship in which man can find the fullness of his being.

Part of the trouble in theological discussion is that we tend to use the word 'God' as though it had the same meaning always and everywhere. This is far from being the case. The idea of God put forward in the Old Testament is not the same as the view to be found in any other ancient religious book. Although Jesus built on the Old Testament, his understanding of God is so revolutionary that when Christians use the word 'God', they mean the Father of our Lord Jesus Christ, and nothing else. God in the Old Testament is, in the main, concerned with a people, though the individual is not neglected; in the New, though the people is not forgotten, God knows and cares for every single individual – 'the very hairs of your head are all numbered' (Luke 12:7). The best pictures of such a God are given in the waiting father of the parable of the prodigal son, and of the good shepherd who goes off to the mountains to find his lost sheep (Luke 15).

Because he believes in such a God as this, Jesus is able to issue without hesitation the most radical and demanding commands.

'Take no anxious thought for the morrow.' This does not by any means imply that God will see to it that everything is snug and comfortable for those who trust in him; Jesus knows all too well that those who believe in him will have to take up their cross and follow him. It does mean that, whatever comes, the Father will be with you in it and will see you through, and in his kingdom nothing is ever wasted. And, after all, Jesus is right. The rich are much more likely than the poor to develop duodenal ulcers, because they have more to be anxious about; if only people could stop being anxious, half the psychiatrists in the country would be out of a job tomorrow.

'Love your enemies.' This is perhaps the most daunting of all the commands, so daunting that many have been inclined to explain it away and to make it mean something other than what it obviously means. The liberal interpretation may be summarised in some such terms as these: 'Do not do more harm than is absolutely necessary to the person whom you dislike, or by whom you feel threatened.' But that is not what Jesus said. The words must be taken in their most literal and exact sense. Your enemy is the man who is out after you with a hatchet to take away your life. Love in the Scriptures, as in the Anglican marriage service, is a word that has surprisingly little emotional content; it means, basically, redemptive action. If a mathematical analysis of 'love' in this sense were to be attempted, it would probably assign ten per cent to emotion; twenty per cent to understanding; seventy per cent to will. Rather surprisingly in the New Testament the word *hetaire*, friend, companion, is used precisely of the one who is acting in a hostile manner, whom you want to win over as your friend. 'Friend, I do thee no wrong,' (Matt. 20:13) is said to the surly labourer in the vineyard, who is discontented with the wages he had agreed to receive. 'Friend, do what you have come to do,' (Matt. 26:50) is the word of Jesus to, of all people, Judas Iscariot. So, if you have an enemy, your job as a Christian is to go to all lengths, even to giving up your life for his, to win him back into friendship. The question whether you like him or not is irrelevant.

Has anyone ever lived like this? Well, the Gospels show that one man did live just like that. The first word of Jesus from the cross was, 'Father, forgive them, for they know not what they do,' (Luke 23:34); this word of Jesus is the basis of all the doctrines of the atonement which have grown up in the life of the Church.

There is a touching story from the period of the American revolutionary war. A Moravian, Peter Miller, had one enemy, who, rebuked by the goodness of a good man, hated him so much that on one occasion he actually spat in his face. Later it came to the good man's notice that his enemy had been captured and sentenced to death as a suspected spy of the English. He made his way into the presence of George Washington himself to ask for a reprieve. The general said, 'I am very sorry, but in the circumstances I do not see my way to spare the life of your friend.' 'My friend!' said the Christian, 'he is the only enemy that I have.' Washington, so the story goes, was so impressed that he issued the desired reprieve.

Such exceptional stories may be few. But it is a fact of experience that, when Muslims have become Christians, the starting-point of their quest has, in many cases, been found to be some act of service rendered by a Christian to a Muslim, who had no claim whatever to any such act of service, the action going far beyond what could ordinarily be expected as between friends. 'The Gospel of the second mile' (Matt. 5:41) does not seem always to make very good sense. But perhaps in the kingdom of God there is something better than good sense.

Difficulties arise when we try to put a precise sense into the word *agape*, love. Paul is in agreement with his Master: 'Love is the fulfilling of the law' (Rom. 13:10). But he was dealing for the most part with raw Gentiles, who had not undergone the discipline of the Jewish law, and came in from that hard, loveless world that is depicted for us in the *Golden Ass* of Apuleius. He found it necessary to instruct them, and so in the second half of a number of his epistles (especially Ephesians and Colossians), laid down a number of ethical precepts. He has been much criticised for doing so, as though he was bringing back law into a world of grace. But these rules are not laws arbitrarily imposed on a situation from without; they are simply an analysis of the meaning of the word *agape*, based on the idea that in Christ we are all one new man, and that he who sins against another sins against himself – not a very sensible thing to do. Paul has at times been criticised as an enemy of the female sex; but has anyone ever written more beautifully than he has written in Ephesians 5 of the relationship between man and woman in marriage? 'This mystery is a profound one, and I am saying that it refers to Christ and the church' (Eph. 5:32 Gk).[7]

One school of experts in the field of morals has propagated what has come to be known as the system of 'situation ethics'.

7. Not all are agreed that the Epistle to the Ephesians was written by Paul himself; but the teaching given in it seems to me profoundly Pauline.

These people lay great stress on *agape*, love, as the principle of all moral action. In doing so they are fully justified both by Scripture and experience. Unfortunately, the strange impression has got about that to follow this 'permissive' school and to make *agape* alone the rule of life, is in some way easier than to follow that analysis of human life and obligation which is contained in the ten commandments and in the teaching of Jesus, as interpreted in the rest of the New Testament. This is exactly the opposite of the truth. The way of *agape* is infinitely more exacting and demanding than the way of the harshest list of rules and commandments. The demands made by rules and laws, however hard, are always limited; it is always possible to say: 'I have done all that was required of me.' The demands made by *agape* are always unlimited. Following the way of *agape* led the Lord Jesus to the cross; there is no reason to suppose that the way of the follower will be any easier than the way of the Master.

And yet, paradoxically, the road of unlimited demand proves to be also the way to unconditional freedom. As it is so beautifully expressed in the third collect at Morning Prayer, 'his service is perfect freedom'.

> *Law informs our ignorance, and when the problem is but obduracy, it will rebuke and condemn. Then the gulf widens and the righteousness of the law goes, by the way of the law, ever further from our reach. If we acquiesce in this situation we are complacent sinners; if we deplore it we are despairing ones. The Gospel of grace is beyond this dilemma of the law. It assures us in the Cross that it reaches beyond our despair, while leaving us no ground for refuge in complacence.*
>
> *Even where it is despised and rejected by the soul of man, the Cross stands majestically. It has a patience and a promise, beyond the competence of law. Its grace will never let us go, as at some point law necessarily must. If we are burdened by the length of human waywardness, as in our*

questions we confessed to being, we shall find in the Cross alone a commensurate enterprise of God for its redemption.
Kenneth Cragg, *Sandals at the Mosque* (1959), pp. 138-9.

3

Teachers East and West - Gautama, Socrates, Jesus

Whom should we follow – eastern teachers who tell us that the world is evil or illusion? Western teachers who tell us to accept the world, because we can do no other? Jesus, who tells us that the world is God's world, and therefore essentially good and serviceable?

Many thoughtful people tell us that religion is primarily experience, that it can never be adequately expressed in words, and that as soon as we try to shut it up in intellectual formulations or rigid doctrinal systems, we destroy its essential nature. There is much truth in this. Religion is far more than doctrine. Some great movements look back to some scintillating example, such as that of Francis of Assisi; others find the best expression of religion in poetry and the beauty of rituals; yet others stress outward observance, like the five Ks passed on to the Sikhs by one of their great Gurus.[1] But history shows that many of those who have most deeply influenced human life did so because they were great teachers; they taught human beings new ways of thinking about life and about the world, and left behind at least outlines of a system of thought, which later generations have had to work out in detail as best they could. Greece, Palestine, India – these great centres of culture – have each left us one supreme teacher, from whose work we can illustrate the view that has here been put forward.

---

1. *Kes,* long hair and beard; *Kangha,* a comb; *Kripan,* a sword or dagger; *Kaccha,* shorts reaching to the knee; *Kara,* a steel arm-band.

Gautama the Buddha stands pre-eminent in the ranks of the religious teachers. Buddhism is a faith of taking refuge; the one who wishes to become a Buddhist has to declare:

I take refuge in the *Buddha* (the Enlightened one)
I take refuge in the *Dhamma* (the teaching)
I take refuge in the *Sangha* (the community).

Quite clearly a parallel declaration could be worked out for the novice in the Christian faith:

I take refuge in the Christ (the light of the world)
I take refuge in the Gospel (the sacred teaching)
I take refuge in the fellowship (the body of Christ the Lord).

The first triad is a summary of what it means to be a Buddhist. The second forms a surprisingly complete summary of what it means to be a Christian.

From the start the ministry of the Buddha showed itself as a ministry of teaching. Having received the great Enlightenment, he sought out the group of ascetics who had deserted him when they felt that he was abandoning the narrow path of strenuous asceticism, and delivered to them the famous Benares sermon. It is not necessary to suppose that the sermon was delivered exactly as it has been recorded, any more than it is necessary to think that the Sermon on the Mount was delivered all in one piece, exactly as it is written down in the Gospel of Matthew. The Buddha's discourse is paradigmatic – it lays down in outline everything that is essential in what has come to be called the Middle Way.[2]

From then on for forty years the life of the Buddha is that of a wandering teacher, the wanderings broken each year by a period in the rainy season when the Teacher gathers his disciples round him for more intensive instruction. He encounters all kinds of people, especially Hindu teachers to whom his new doctrine is likely to seem unattractive; in these long arguments the thread of Buddhist discourse is skilfully woven, until it becomes a rope too stout to be unpicked by the

2. Middle Way, as lying between self-indulgent life in the world, and the utter self-denial of extreme asceticism.

hands of those less skilled in the art of dialectic. All these discourses are to be found in the many volumes bearing in English the title, *Dialogues of the Buddha.*

It is possible to dip into these volumes at almost any point, and find something that relates to the very heart of Buddhist doctrine. For instance, we find a somewhat lengthy dialogue with a mendicant named Potthapādu, which turns on the doctrine of the soul. Towards the end of the dialogue, the Buddha says, 'That, Potthapādu, is a matter on which I have expressed no opinion'; to a number of other questions, he gives the same answer. When Potthapādu asks, 'But why has the Exalted One expressed no opinion on that?', the answer is given, 'This question is not calculated to profit, it is not concerned with the *Dhamma*, it does not resound even to the elements of right conduct, nor to detachment, nor to purification from lusts, nor to quietude, nor to tranquillisation of heart, nor to real knowledge, nor to true insight, nor to *Nirvāna*. Therefore it is that I expressed no opinion on it.' 'Then what is it that the Exalted One has determined?' 'I have expounded, Potthapādu, what pain is; I have expounded what is the origin of pain; I have expounded what is the cessation of pain; I have expounded what is the method by which one may reach the cessation of pain . . .' 'That is so, O Excellent One, that is so, O Happy One. And now let the Exalted One do what seemeth to him fit.'[3]

So it goes on through endless pages, patient, courteous, humorous. The arguments of the Buddha are not on the whole convincing to the western consciousness, since they contain far too many unproved assumptions. But over the centuries they have developed a stalwart tower of Buddhist orthodoxy, which the arguments of Christians have found it singularly difficult to penetrate.

The East looks to one great teacher. The West looks to another who was born in Athens just about the time of the

3. T.W. Rhys Davids, *Dialogues of the Buddha* (Part I, ed. of 1956), pp. 241-65.

death of the Buddha. If Aristotle is, as Dante hailed him, the master of those who know, and Plato is the master of those who think, Socrates is without doubt the master of those who teach. His name is preserved in the Socratic method of teaching, which claims to be modelled on the example he set. When we read Plato, it is never possible to be sure how much actual Socrates we have, and how much is due to the brilliant disciple, who at times elaborated what he had heard and exercised his own originality in the doctrine that he sets before us. But in the marvellous pictures that Plato draws of the cool walks by the Ilissos, and of the changing-room where the young men resort after their races and their wrestling and meet their friends, much of the atmosphere of Athens two thousand four hundred years ago comes across; we feel that we are listeners in on the extraordinarily varied conversations that are provided for our entertainment.

The *Symposium* for example, with its brilliant delineation of each one of the participants, leading up to the great discourse of the priestess Diotima, which guides the reader from the lesser forms of love up to the heavenly love of that which truly is, gives the impression of an evening of hilarity, which ends in accents of the utmost seriousness. The final scene, in the *Phaedo*, where Socrates takes leave of his friends in the prison, with its touches of humour, is among the most moving passages in human literature; well did the friends record that they had lost the best of men, and for all in all the wisest and most righteous of the human race.

Socrates always takes the position of the one who is wise because he knows that he knows nothing, a pose which is at times irritating, but which finds its justification in the bland assumption made by human beings that they know many things of which thay have no more than a vague and fleeting idea. The dialectic in a number of passages proves arid and tedious. But the aim is always serious. The sophist, with his airs of superior knowledge, must be deflated. The average honest man must be shown how superficial is his ordinary way of thinking. But there is always the assumption that the pearl of truth lies not very far hidden from our eyes, unless indeed we are disqualified by the 'lie in the soul' from any earnest seeking. It is for this reason that we turn endlessly to Plato for warning against superficiality, for condemnation of slip-shod methods, for delicate humour and satire, for brilliant areas of poetry, for occasional blinding flashes of truth. It is not so much that we believe what Plato wants us to believe, as that we rise from the study of him, chastened and braced to 'follow the argument as far as ever it will go', and to 'save the phenomena', to be discontented with half-hearted explanations that do not wrestle with the whole complex reality that confronts us.

The great teacher from the East and the great teacher from the West are at one in sharing in one notable characteristic to be found in all the greatest teachers – intense seriousness. The Buddha turns aside from definition and discussion of many things that are irrelevant to his concern with deliverance, that taste which, as he says, is to be found in all the Buddhist teachings as the taste of salt is to be found in all the seven seas. Socrates, as depicted by Plato, though his discourses wander through many and varied fields, is all the time concerned about one thing only – that the truth should appear. But they are alike in one other thing – the teaching of each is ultimately a world-denying doctrine.

To the Buddha all outward things are only distractions. They have no ultimate reality; they belong to a universe of illusion, from which the seeker must desire to be freed. What is set before the Buddhist aspirant is the noble eightfold path; the eighth of the rules set before him is right meditation. Meditation will draw him inwards and away from all these outward things; it will set him free from the complexity of thought into a world of simplicity; it will lead him to doubt or to deny the reality of his own existence; so it will draw him nearer to that final and ultimate peace of Nirvāna, cessation from all being, or at least from every kind of being that is conceivable by the unillumined mind.

Plato is keenly sensitive to the beauty and interest of the world. Yet those beings which inhabit the visible world have only appearance without reality. In regard to all such things, it is possible to have opinion, but not knowledge. To have correct opinion is, of course, far better than to have mistaken opinion; but it remains opinion, and not to be confused with knowledge. Those who remain in this world of opinion are, in the most famous of all Plato's similitudes, like inhabitants of a cave, who do not see real objects, but only the shadows of the objects cast on the wall of the cave to which their eyes are directed. *Knowledge* can only be of unchanging realities, of the forms, the essential substances, which underlie every individual manifestation. So Plato leads us away from visible reality into the world of the forms, and at the head and summit of these forms is the idea or form of the Good, the ultimate truth after which the wise man must aspire. But, when we ask Plato to put content into this abstract and remote reality, he finds it hard to meet our desire. What is this form of the Good? It can be apprehended only by those who have made the pilgrimage from appearance to reality, and perhaps they will find no words in which to explain what it is to those who have never made the same pilgrimage.

Jesus belonged neither to the eastern nor to the western tradition. If we compare him with either of the great teachers of whom we have been speaking, with regard to seriousness or to concern for the manifestation of the truth, he will emerge from the comparison as at least the equal of both. But, on closer inspection, he diverges radically from their views. His roots are in the Old Testament and in the Hebrew tradition. The first words of the Bible are, 'In the beginning God created the heavens and the earth.' The basis of all the teaching of Jesus is the affirmation of the world. God made it and it is good. The visible world is real. Its reality is indeed not absolute but contingent, since it is every moment dependent on God; it has no reality apart from him. But it is neither illusion nor deception.

This means that Jesus's understanding of the world is sacramental – to use the language of the Anglican catechism, it is the outward and visible sign of an inward and spiritual grace.

Visible things, in their beauty and order, reveal, though not perfectly, the One in whom they have their origin. Moreover the world is a place of real happenings, happenings that are significant both for time and for eternity. It is a place in which great issues are decided – issues of good and evil, of righteousness and unrighteousness, of perdition and salvation. In all of these the destinies of the human race, and of every human being, are involved.

Jesus was born into a world in which teaching was regarded as being of great importance. As prophetic inspiration died away, the place of the prophet was taken by the teacher, the learned in the law who could expound scripture to the less learned, and make known the will of God for his people. The great prophets were followed by the great Rabbis. Much of the rabbinic teaching seems to non-Jews to be antiquated and obscure, sometimes even trivial. But through the troubled period that led up to the days of Jesus, and far onward into the Christian period, Jewish history is illuminated by the names of really great teachers, who maintained the faith, elaborated doctrine, and kept alive among the people the hope of better days, since it was unthinkable that God could ever permanently forsake his people. Almost inevitably, when Jesus stood before the people with his proclamation of God's kingdom and his righteousness, one of the titles bestowed upon him was precisely the title Rabbi, teacher; this came to be the way in which his followers in the early days addressed him.

This use of the title involved two perplexities. In the first place it was clear that Jesus had not passed through the regular curriculum of studies which would entitle the student to claim the title Rabbi. 'How is it that this man has learning, when he has never studied?' (John 7:15) was the question to which the learned of Jerusalem could find no immediately satisfactory answer. It was evident that he could hold his own in discussion and dialectic with the experts in the law, and seemed never to be at a loss for a reply to the questions that were put to him. Could native shrewdness take the place of the sometimes tedious instruction of the schools?

The perplexity experienced by the common people was of a different kind. He spoke with authority. This was the first comment recorded by Mark in the course of the first encounter of Jesus with the hearers in the synagogue: 'What is this? It is a new doctrine invested with power' (Mark 1:27 Gk). Perhaps the wide variations in the Greek manuscripts at this point reflect the uncertainty experienced by the hearers. But Matthew, as is his custom, adds a fuller explanation for the benefit of those who stood at a rather greater remove from the original occurrences: 'When Jesus had brought all these words to an end, the crowds of hearers were absolutely astonished at his teachings; for it was his habit to teach them as one possessing authority, and not as their own learned men' (Matt. 7:28-29 Gk). This correctly reflects Jewish, and indeed Islamic, tradition. The credibility of a saying, or a piece of teaching, depends upon the genealogy of its tradition, of the way it has been transmitted from mouth to mouth, so that it can be traced back to one to whom great authority has been generally ascribed. Jesus must have known many of these traditions, but he does not rest on them, indeed at times criticises them; he speaks directly from fresh springs of inspiration, and these give him the power to speak with innate and underived authority.

When he wishes to refer to any existing authority, it is to the Old Testament that Jesus looks. The synagogues played a notable part in the life of the Jewish people, and the schools attached to them kept alive a tradition of popular learning such as among Greeks and Romans was the possession of only a select few. Hebrew was no longer a generally spoken language; in synagogue worship ordinary people would need the service of the interpreter, who would render the lessons out of the original Hebrew into the Aramaic which was more generally understood. But the differences between Hebrew and Aramaic are less than those between Latin and Norman French; for an intelligent student, such as we may suppose Jesus to have been, the mastery of the Old Testament in Hebrew would not have been an excessively difficult task. It is clear that the ancient words dwelt in his heart and on his lips.

What distinguished him from other interpreters was the blessed gift of imagination. These are not dead words from a long distant past; they sparkle with life and revelation. The question of the resurrection of the dead was a well-worn subject for debates in the schools; Jesus unerringly puts his finger on the relevant passage which the conservative Sadducees, no less than the more tolerant Pharisees, will accept as binding. It occurs in the passage known as 'The Bush', where God, speaking to Moses, refers to himself as 'the God of Abraham and the God of Isaac and the God of Jacob', to which Jesus adds the comment, 'He is not the God of the dead, but of the living' (Mark 12:26-27). It is he who finds in the often obscure text of the prophet Hosea the great utterance which in Matthew he is reported as having cited twice: 'My desire is for mercy and not for sacrifice' (Matt. 9:13, 12:7). To this, in the latter passage, is appended the comment of Jesus, 'if they had understood the passage, they would not have condemned those who were in no way worthy of blame'. The Old Testament law is not to be allowed to become a burden too heavy for man to bear; the sabbath was given for rest for man and for beast; hedged round by Pharisaic rules it had become a day of anxious scruples and not a day for liberty and for rejoicing.

The Old Testament plays an important part, but only a part, in the teaching of Jesus. The freshness of that teaching comes in no small measure from the vivid pictures that it draws from the daily scene in the Palestine of his days. He is alert to the beauty of the scarlet anemones[4] that deck the fields in the short Palestinian spring, to the birds of the air, not excluding the vultures that gather where carrion has been scented from afar. He is familiar with the traveller traversing the dangerous road from Jericho to Jerusalem on his donkey; with the labourer who bears the burden and heat of a long day in the vineyards; with the passers-by in the temple, from the familiar figure of

---

4. Though some would include such flowers as poppies, gladioli and irises in a wider interpretation of the term.

the Pharisee who was so very well pleased with himself to the widow whose gift was so small that she may have thrust it almost surreptitiously into the large vessel waiting to receive it. All these scenes and characters have become proverbial; familiarity may have hidden from us the extent to which this style of teaching was original, with hardly a direct parallel in the teaching of the Jewish Rabbis.

One feature in the teaching of Jesus recurs so frequently that it may be described as generally characteristic of his method. He is slow to give answers, but, like Socrates, very ready to ask questions; but in many cases the question is put in such a way that the one who is required to answer finds that he already has the answer to the question which he himself has previously posed.

One of the best known of all the parables of Jesus is the story of the good Samaritan who helped the traveller lying wounded by the wayside after his encounter with robbers. A lawyer, wishing to test the capacity of Jesus to deal with a matter of doubt, has posed the question: 'Who is my neighbour?' The question is not quite as straightforward as it might appear. The command to 'love thy neighbour as thyself' is taken from the book of Leviticus in the Old Testament (19:18). There it almost certainly has the restricted meaning 'your fellow Israelite'. Is Jesus maintaining this restriction, or is he setting it on one side in favour of a more universal understanding of the command? Jesus deliberately chooses a Samaritan as the hero of his story. Relations between Jews and Samaritans were in general stormy, to say the least; in fact we are told in the fourth Gospel that Jews have no dealings with Samaritans (4:9). The Samaritan was the very one who might have been expected to pass by on the other side and to take no notice of the wounded man. There is a certain subtlety in the question Jesus puts to the lawyer: 'Who do you think played the part of a neighbour to the one who had fallen into the hands of the robbers?' (in the Greek, it is 'became neighbour', 'made himself neighbour'). Inevitably the lawyer is bound to answer, 'the one who showed kindness to him' – he has himself the answer to the question with which he had approached Jesus.

Perhaps there is a further subtlety in the tale as Jesus tells it. When do you discover who your neighbour is? Not when you are in a position to render help to one who is in need, but when you yourself are in desperate need, and looking round anxiously for a helping hand. You are the wounded man by the roadside; in your need you are not likely to pay much attention to the question whether your helper is 'Jew, Turk, infidel or heretic'[5], or whoever else he may happen to be.

Jesus was in the habit of welcoming the approach of those whom society was inclined to cast out as undesirables. On one occasion a woman of notoriously irregular life drew near to him as he was reclining at a banquet. Jesus, aware of disapproving looks, told one of the shortest and simplest of his parables, that of the two debtors to both of whom the creditor remitted the debt which each had incurred. Which of the two will be most grateful to the generous creditor? (Our experts in the Aramaic language tell us that this is the meaning of the word 'love' in this connection.) The answer is too obvious to be evaded; as Jesus has expressed it in another connection, those who are whole have no need of a physician, but those who are sick. 'She loved much' should be translated 'she has shown by her actions the extent of her gratitude' (Luke 7:36-50).[6]

The same teaching underlies the story of the two sons, neither of whom brought much happiness to his father. The occasion of the parable is clearly set out – tax-gatherers and other disreputable people had collected in crowds to hear the words of Jesus, and as usual objections were raised by those who had a rather good opinion of themselves. The figure of the younger son is highly picturesque, and he draws most of the attention of the reader; but the elder son is perhaps even more striking as an example of brilliant portraiture. He speaks only

---

5. This phrase will be readily recognised by those who are familiar with the Anglican Book of Common Prayer.

6. For a superb exposition of this story, see S. Kierkegaard, *Christian Discourses*, pp. 379-86.

once (even those who believe themselves to know the Bible well might be hard put to it to quote his utterance correctly), but each of the four clauses of which he delivers himself is a complete give-away of the cantankerous and self-righteous man. He is unprepared to refer to the castaway as 'my brother'; – 'he is your son, and you can have him as far as I am concerned'. With exquisite art, whether of Jesus who told the parable or of Luke who recorded it, the story breaks off at a culminating point – 'this thy brother was dead and has come to life, was lost and is found'. Each of the characters stands out so clearly that no comment is needed; there is no need for Jesus to explain who it is that is delineated in the character of the father in the story.

Sometimes a question arises out of a point that has been raised earlier in a conversation. Two disciples, looking forward to the coming of the kingdom of which Jesus has so often spoken, are desirous to secure for themselves a pre-eminent place in that kingdom. The question is couched in somewhat mysterious terms: 'Are you able to drink the cup that I drink or to be baptised with the baptism with which I am baptised?' (Mark 10:38). As so often in Mark's Gospel, the shadow of suffering and death falls across the page. With almost fatuous simplicity the two disciples make the affirmation, 'We can'. He welcomes their profession of loyalty, even though they may not have understood how harshly that loyalty is to be tested in the not-very-distant future.

At times, Jesus skilfully draws a conversation forward to the point that he has in mind, and sums it up in a phrase of capital importance. The discussion which Jesus holds with a woman of Samaria is brilliantly dramatic; but her successive evasions do not hold him back from coming to the essential issue, and to the affirmation that God is Spirit, and that those who worship him must worship him in spirit and in truth (John 4:24).

The teachings of Jesus are episodic – they arise out of actual situations, and are related to the needs of individuals. For this reason they cannot be systematised or reduced to a manual of theology. There are, however, certain recurrent themes, under which it is possible to group a number of his sayings, at least into outlines of a system.

First and foremost are the sayings which have direct reference to God. This God is the God of Abraham, Isaac and Jacob. It is in the midst of the people of the Jews that Jesus bears witness. His own ministry is limited to that particular people; he guards himself against the danger of dissipating his resources by going too far afield, and welcomes only those Gentiles who show by their faith that they are qualified to be counted among the chosen people. But the way in which he speaks of God breaks through the barriers of narrowness and sectarianism; this is the God who makes his sun to shine on the evil and the good, and is kind to the unthankful and the evil (Matt. 5:45).

One of the features of the character of God as shown in the Old Testament is faithfulness. He is a God who can be relied on, the God who keeps his covenant with the whole race of man and in particular with his chosen people. This is intensified in the teaching of Jesus. God can be depended upon in every circumstance of life. He knows intimately the needs of those who put their trust in him; he sees the sparrow fall from the nest; and 'ye are of more value than many sparrows' (Luke 12:7).

Central in the teaching of Jesus is the idea of the kingdom of God. The balance of the world has been upset by the ravages of sin; now God himself will intervene and take charge, and restore all things to what they were intended to be according to his good purpose. The 'miracles' of Jesus are not casual manifestations of power or of goodwill to those in need. They are signs of the presence of the kingdom, signs of the restoration of the normal through the intervention of God's healing power. The withered hand is restored to normal use. The leper, segregated by Jewish law from society, is brought back again into the fellowship of men. More important than any other sign is the proclamation of the good news to the poor – those who are literally poor in that they lack their due share of the good things of life, but also those who, according to Old

Testament usage, put their whole trust and confidence in God, and wait for the manifestation of his power.

Jesus has no doubt that this sovereign rule of God is present because he is present. This must be the meaning of the saying, often misunderstood, that 'the kingdom of heaven is in your midst'; where Jesus is, there the rule of God is visibly present. This kingdom may come suddenly, when men are least expecting it: 'If I by the finger of God cast out demons, then the kingdom of God has come upon you' (Luke 11:20).

This understanding of himself accounts for one other among the many paradoxes which make the figure of Jesus always in a measure mysterious. There is the humility which enables him to become the servant of everyone, dramatically shown in the episode in the fourth Gospel in which Jesus literally takes the form of a servant, and performs the servile ministration of washing the disciples' feet. Those who follow the one who was in the midst of the disciples as one who serves, must equally make themselves the servants of all. Yet with all this there is the other side – the calm, unquestioning authority with which he issues his commands. The call to follow him is issued unconditionally, it demands obedience. For many the call is too hard; they follow so far, but then turn back and walk in a different way. For those who follow all the way there is no reward other than the satisfaction of being caught up in a glorious enterprise, and of sharing in the companionship of the one they have chosen to follow.

Nothing is plainer in the teaching of Jesus than the affirmation that to follow him is to choose his way of suffering. Already in the New Testament there is clear evidence that Jesus had not exaggerated the danger. Paul is our first-hand witness. In 2 Corinthians 11 he gives a grim list of the sufferings that he had endured at the hands of both Jews and Romans. By the time at which the Gospels came to be written down, the hostility of the Jews had settled into steady enmity, and the Romans were being increasingly drawn into the quarrel. We may think that the evangelists were to some extent drawing on more recent experience, and so were adding vivid detail to the picture which Jesus had originally drawn, but there is no reason to suppose that they were simply inventing; the teacher had given the warning; when events turned out as he had said they would, the followers naturally remembered what he had said, and recalled warnings to which, when they were originally uttered, they had perhaps rendered no more than cursory attention.

This chapter opened with a brief consideration of two great teachers, one from the Indian and one from the Greek tradition. The chapter may appropriately end with the problem of suffering, and of the attitudes towards it adopted by each of the three great teachers with whose views and methods we have been occupied through the greater part of this chapter.

In a celebrated passage in the second book of the *Republic*, Plato pictures the perfectly good man appearing in human society, and the horrifying things that may happen to him, if society is misled into confusing good with evil. The story as he tells it corresponds so perfectly with what actually happened in history, that not surprisingly Christians who read the *Republic* attributed to Plato almost miraculous foresight.

Glaucon is depicting for the sake of argument the superbly unrighteous man who succeeds in earning a great reputation for righteousness, and by contrast with him the truly good man who yet is reckoned among the unrighteous. This is what he says:

> We must strip the righteous man of everything except his righteousness. He does nothing wrong, but let him acquire an overwhelming reputation for wrongdoing ... let him continue unshaken in his course, even up to the point of death, all through his life appearing to be unrighteous, though in point of fact he is righteous ... So we have two of very different nature, and in my opinion it will not be difficult to foretell the kind of life which each may expect ... Those who commend unrighteousness in preference to righteousness will say that the righteous man will be flogged and tortured, bound with chains, will have his eyes burned

> out, and when he has endured every kind of suffering will finally be impaled, and so he will learn that what we should choose is not to be righteous but to have the reputation of being righteous. (*Republic,* II, p. 361 B–E).

The problem with which Socrates is dealing throughout the *Republic* is just this: Why is it better to be good than to be bad? He is unwavering in his view that, in spite of all arguments to the contrary, the good is always to be chosen. This resolute preference of the good, literally at all costs, entitles Socrates, and his disciple Plato, to be reckoned among the great teachers of mankind.

The problem of the suffering of the apparently innocent has perplexed Indian thinkers, both Hindu and Buddhist, from the beginning of time. The Buddha, like Plato, recognises the inevitability of suffering in human life, but his way of handling it is very different. Everything in life is suffering – to lose that which one values, and to be joined with that which one detests; sickness is suffering, old age is suffering, death is suffering. Suffering arises from desire. Cut the root of desire, and we shall cut the root of suffering. In order to make the operation as radical as it can well be made, we will annihilate the self, and with that destruction of the illusion of a self we shall destroy also that illusion of suffering by which human beings are distressed.

So the end of all things is cessation – that *Nirvāna* which to the Buddhist brings release. The more ruthless among the expositors of *Nirvāna* maintain that it means absolute nothingness. Any form of existence, however it may be imagined, will be accompanied by suffering. Why then should I desire any kind of existence? To cease to be is far more desirable than any other end. In the meantime, the wise man will attain to a calm serenity of expectation. He will look out on the ignorance and the sufferings of human beings with passionless goodwill; but he will not allow himself to be in any way emotionally engaged, since such engagement would tie him again to the wheel of passion, detachment from which is the aim of all his striving.

In contrast to these two great thinkers and teachers, the attitude of Jesus to suffering is almost startling in its ordinariness. Here is neither the high-powered rhetoric of Plato nor the subtlety of Gautama. Jesus calmly accepts suffering as part of human life. It is not to be sought; to run into unnecessary suffering is pathological. But it is never to be evaded at the cost of a surrender of conscience. If suffering comes, the disciples are to be neither surprised nor dismayed nor resentful. This is something that simply has to be accepted, in the belief that it can serve as discipline and training, and by the power of God can be elevated into an experience in which the full splendour of what it means to be human can be displayed. This quality of ordinariness runs through much of the teaching of Jesus. It is this, perhaps, which has given to his words their extraordinary power to move the hearts of men and women through almost twenty centuries.

Plato and Gautama were aristocrats. Gautama came of princely lineage; through all the records he marches as a most superior person. His doctrine has been kept alive through a particular aristocracy, the religious orders of monks and nuns. There are forms of Buddhism, especially in its northern forms, which are available to very ordinary people, but to wrestle with the intricacies of Buddhist metaphysics is to enter a world in which by comparison the greater part of western philosophy is so simple as to appear almost naïve. Plato was a citizen of a highly aristocratic city, in which citizens were few, and all the heavier work was done by slaves. The charming young men who appear in the dialogues belonged to a leisured class, in which there was always time to hear some new thing, to sit at the feet of the latest sophist, by whom, in the judgment of Socrates, their intellectual integrity was in danger of being despoiled. Plato's later thinking leads us into a difficult world of thought, in which the soldier, sailor, tinker, tailor cannot readily find themselves at home.

Jesus was no aristocrat; he was an ordinary man. In his day Palestine was a very small country; but the Gospels present us with an almost Shakespearian amphitheatre of human experience. Jesus was moving about all the time and meeting all kinds of people – rulers and ordinary citizens, the richer and the poorer, religious teachers, peasants and fishermen, women of the streets and respectable matrons, little children and young men of promise, animals and birds. Much of his teaching arises out of the most ordinary human situations; the greatest of his parables emerges from the harsh criticism voiced by his enemies; another from the contemptuous attitude of the self-righteous to a poor convicted woman. What is not ordinary is the depth of his awareness of the human situation – in its greatness and its misery. The simplest of his stories, like the clear waters of a deep, still pool, reveal depth upon depth of meaning, hidden from those who are not willing to take the trouble to look into the depths. He knew what was in man.

The sceptical French scholar, Ernest Renan, remarked that the Gospel according to St Luke was the most beautiful book ever written. Was he perhaps right? Frances Cornford the poetess, a grand-daughter of Charles Darwin, had been brought up to believe that religion was good for some people but not for Darwins. When her extraordinarily beautiful children began to ask awkward questions about religion, she thought she had better find out about things and turned to the New Testament. Not very much later she remarked to a friend, 'Mr Angus, I have been reading the Gospels, and I find that the things Jesus said about God are true.'

Was she right? The natural sciences have revealed to us that things which appear simple may on analysis prove to be incredibly complex. Modern psychology has shown us that we ourselves are far more complex than perhaps we had realised, that human personality is an amazingly intricate structure, which even now we are only beginning to understand. So intellectual eminence is not to be despised; the thinkers who bring hidden depths of knowledge to light are always to be revered. But perhaps the greatest teachers of all are those who can find for the most profound truths the simplest form of expression. Does not the supremacy of Jesus as teacher lie just in this – that his greatest utterances are also often his simplest? And is it not often the case that apparently very simple people have a native shrewdness which leads them to the very heart of what he has to say?

The story is told of an elderly woman in Scotland, who when tested by her minister as to her fitness to become a full member of the Church, cried out, 'Sir, I cannot answer all your hard questions. All I know is that I would gladly die for him.'

She knew the meaning of the words, 'Follow me'.

So it was when Jesus came in his gentleness
With his divine compassion and great Gospel of Peace,
men hail'd him WORD OF GOD, and in the title of Christ
crown'd him with love beyond all earthly names of renown.
For He, wandering unarm'd save by the Spirit's flame,
in few years with few friends founded a world-empire
wider than Alexander's and more enduring;
since from his death it took its everlasting life.
HIS kingdom is God's kingdom, and his holy temple
not in Athens or Rome, but in the heart of man.

Robert Bridges, *The Testament of Beauty,* I. 771-780.

4

A True Prophet: or More than a Prophet?

We need not doubt that Muhammad was a prophet for his people and for his day. But does he offer us all that we need in the late twentieth century?

Prophets are perplexing creatures. They seem to appear out of nowhere, and sometimes disappear again into nowhere. Some who announce themselves to be prophets are rather insignificant people, and, because they achieve no resonance in the minds of their contemporaries, have only limited influence, if any influence at all, Others, however, do radiate a strange spiritual power, and convince some at least among their hearers that they have received a divine message, which they must at all costs pass on to those who are willing to listen. An excellent definition of what it means to be a prophet is given by the Swedish bishop, Tor Andrae, in his sensitive study of *Mohammed: The Man and his Faith* (p.52):

A genuine prophet is one who really has a message to deliver, one in whose soul some of the great questions of his age have stimulated a restlessness which compels him to speak, and for whom the ecstasy and prophetic inspiration are but the natural and inevitable expression of a strong lasting conviction and a genuine passion.

The main difference between the prophetic and the priestly types of religion is that the priest has credentials to offer, and the prophet has none. For a man to be a priest in the Jewish tradition, it was necessary that he belong to the tribe of Levi, and that he be a lineal descendant of one of the branches of the Aaronic family. As the Epistle to the Hebrews correctly notes, Jesus, being of the tribe of Judah, had no claim to be a member of the Aaronic priesthood. An Anglican priest, if challenged, can produce his letters of Orders, showing when and where he was ordained to the office, and thereby received accreditation for the performance of those functions in the Church that belong to that office. The prophet has nothing of the kind to produce.

If the function of the prophet is identified with prediction of the future, which is certainly one aspect of the prophetic office, a practical test can very easily be applied: 'When a prophet speaks in the name of the Lord, if the word does not come to pass or come true, that is a word which the Lord has not spoken; the prophet has spoken it presumptuously, you need not be afraid of him' (Deut. 18:22). The prophet Jeremiah was greatly afflicted by rivals in the prophetic profession, who 'healed the wound of my people lightly, saying "Peace, peace," when there is no peace' (Jer, 8:11). When Hananiah, the son of Azzur, announces that the Lord of hosts has broken the yoke of the king of Babylon, Jeremiah can only answer, 'Amen! May the Lord do so; may the Lord make the words which you have prophesied come true' (Jer. 28:5-9). He knows that Hananiah is speaking falsely in the name of the Lord, but for the moment it is just the word of one prophet against another; only the day will declare the truth of the one and the deceitfulness of the other.

If, however, we understand the work of the prophet in a wider sense, as serving as the mouthpiece of a living God, then there is another criterion which can be applied – the sensitive recognition of the reality of prophetic power.

How, then, is it possible to distinguish the false from the true? The authority of the true prophet depends on nothing other than the intrinsic power of his utterance, and the intensity of his conviction that the words he speaks are not his own, but have come to him from some superior or supernatural power. So, when Jesus is challenged as to the authority on which he acts, his reference to John the Baptist is not a clever evasion of the difficulty, but a legitimate answer which is directly on the target (Mark 11:27-33). Those who are spiritually sensitive will respond to the prophet's message and will recognise the source from which his authority is derived. If the questioners were too obtuse to be aware that John was an authentic prophet speaking in the name of the Lord, it could not be expected that they would be aware of the One in whose name Jesus was speaking and of the divine power that flowed through his words.

Jews and Christians are most familiar with the prophetic figures who appear in the pages of the Old Testament. But it is not necessary to suppose that so divine a gift flowed only through one single stream; we should, perhaps, be ready to recognise that other peoples also have had their prophetic figures, and that the authority that flowed through them, though perhaps not comparable with that which was manifest in the Israelite prophets, was at least in its own measure genuine.

Most students of the subject would be prepared to admit that Zarathustra was in his day a prophet to the people of Iran. The Parsis today are a rather small community in India, and without doubt the faith which they profess has undergone many and various developments in the course of more than two millennia. But that faith they derive from one who is believed to have spoken with authority at roughly the same period of history as the writing prophets of the Old Testament. It is difficult to speak confidently of Zarathustra, in part by reason of the extreme obscurity of the *Gāthās*, the poems which make up the oldest stratum of Zoroastrian literature, and the difficulty of which is such that the labours of devoted generations of interpreters are very far from having carried them to unanimity. It seems possible, however, to state with some confidence that Zarathustra was born somewhere about the year 620 BC, in the northern or eastern section of the country now called Iran. His message seems to reflect the unsettled social conditions of the time, inasmuch as he identifies the good with the settled pastoral and agricultural peoples, whereas the followers of 'the Lie' are the raiders who disrupt orderly and settled life, and have nothing satisfactory to put in its place.

The main lines of the teaching of Zarathustra do seem to be identifiable, though not at all points with certainty. He makes a passionate claim on behalf of the one, single, good spirit, as against the lords many and gods many who divided the allegiance of his contemporaries. There is a secondary power, Angro Mainyu (Ahriman), which is hostile to the supreme good spirit, Ahura Mazda (Ormuzd); men must choose to which side they will adhere. There will come a day of judgment, on which human beings will have to cross the narrow bridge, *cinvat peretu*; the virtuous will be able to cross it, though with difficulty, and enter into paradise; the impious will fall down into everlasting perdition. One of the emphases of Zarathustra is on the pure and divine element of the sacred fire. Parsis very much object to being called fire-worshippers; they do not worship the fire, but treasure it and keep it alight, as the precious and incomparable symbol of the divine.

If this brief summary comes anywhere near to catching the significance of what Zarathustra taught, it is clear that there was a certain noble simplicity about his teaching; two ways are set before man, and with them a certain inevitability of choice. One modern writer has affirmed without hesitation that 'Zoroaster was one of the greatest religious geniuses of all time'.[1]

For all that, the message of Zarathustra is limited both in extent and in depth. One of the most sympathetic of his modern expositors, Nathan Söderblom, has stated that 'Zarathustra had not fathomed the misery of human life nor the secret of evil ... Neither the corruptibility and

1. R.C. Zaehner in *Concise Encyclopaedia of Living Faiths* (1959), p.222.

vanity of existence nor distress of soul had brought him to the critical point when self-confidence and the natural man are slain and man is born, if it so be, to a new existence'.[2]

Of the prophet of the Arabs, we know a great deal more, and can obtain a reasonably clear image of the man and of his message. Through a good many centuries Christians were in the habit of dismissing Muhammad simply as 'the false prophet'. A change set in on Friday, 8 March 1840, when Thomas Carlyle in his second lecture on 'Heroes and Hero Worship' introduced the Hero as prophet. To Carlyle, Muhammad was a man of immense seriousness; he had glimpsed something of the divine light – 'a confused dazzling splendour of life and heaven, in the great darkness which threatened to be death; he called it revelation and the angel Gabriel – who of us yet can know what to call it?' Many since Carlyle have tried to understand the secret and the greatness of Muhammad.

The prophetic call of Muhammad seems not to have come to him till his fortieth year (AD 611), when he received the command, 'Recite.' His experience of revelation came to him with great intensity of feeling. According to one of the traditions, he replied in answer to a question relating to his revelations, 'I hear loud noises, and then it seems as if I am struck by a blow. I never receive a revelation without the consciousness that my soul is being taken away from me.' According to another tradition Ayesha, the prophet's favourite wife, averred that she had seen how the revelation came to the Apostle on a very cold day, and that when it was completed his brow dripped with perspiration. From this some have inferred that Muhammad was an epileptic; this inference rests on no good evidence. It is clear that the Prophet was, as was said of the philosopher Spinoza, a God-intoxicated man; his religious experience may have been narrow, but it was profound.

---

2. *The Living God* (1933), pp.210-11.

Christians should read the Koran. But, if they are approaching it without previous knowledge, they should be advised to read it backwards. When the collection was made, the chapters were arranged in order of length, and this means that those which come first in the collected order belong to the latest sections of the ministry of Muhammad, while the shorter utterances which come at the end belong to the earlier period when his ministry was exercised in Mecca. The last fifty-seven chapters cover, in Sale's translation, only fifty-seven pages, as against three hundred and sixty pages for the first fifty-seven. In these earlier chapters a great deal of the essential teaching of Muhammad is to be found.

Some of these oracles are extremely short, not more than two or three lines, in this resembling the oracles of several Old Testament prophets, which were afterwards collected by their disciples in the form in which we have them. Such short oracles are highly pregnant in meaning. On the unbeliever, 'Say: O unbelievers, I will not worship that which ye worship: nor will ye worship that which I worship. Neither do I worship that which ye worship; neither do ye worship that which I worship. Ye have your religion, and I my religion' (Sura cix). At times the incantations with which chapters open are almost eerie in their solemnity. 'By the war-horses which run swiftly to the battle, with a panting noise, and by those which strike fire by dashing their hooves against the stones' (Sura c). 'By the brightness of the morning; and by the night, when it groweth dark: thy Lord hath not forsaken thee, neither doth he hate thee' (Sura xciii). 'By the sun, and its rising brightness; by the moon when she followeth him; by the day, when it showeth his splendour; by the night when it covereth him with darkness; by the heaven and by him who built it; by the earth, and him who spread it forth; by the ground and him who moulded it' (Sura xci). Those who can read Arabic tell us that much of the splendour of the original is lost in even the best of translations, but it is clear that this is an original style, deservedly called prophetic.

When the Prophet was asked to sum up his teaching in few

words, he stated that it had to do with God and the day of judgment. To these two themes he recurs constantly; the day of judgment is a terrible and imminent reality; there will be no intercession and no mercy; for the unbeliever there is no possible fate other than that of being cast into the eternal fires of hell. And belief can be summed up in the single clause, 'I declare that there is no God but God'. Muhammad was disgusted by the idolatry that he found practised in Mecca and among the surrounding Bedouin tribes. He seems to have come under the influence of both Judaism and Christianity and to have learned from those religions a doctrine of monotheism, which he accepted in its starkest and most uncompromising form, and declared with the intensity of a consuming passion.

There is something noble in the picture of the solitary man, holding forth the truth as he has seen it for thirteen years, making hardly a single convert other than his wife, Khadijah. There is much in his later life that is unattractive to the Christian reader. There is, however, no need to be doubtful of the reality of his prophetic vision, and of the sincerity with which he proclaimed it, 'Whether they would hear or whether they would forbear'. Can a Christian be satisfied with this revelation of the being of God? Or does he find that he has to look elsewhere for the answer to questions about God which are neither raised nor answered in the Koran?

The prophetic type was familiar in the Semitic world. It is not surprising that, when Jesus exercised his brief ministry in Galilee and Judaea, the people took it for granted that he stood in the ancient and familiar lineage of the prophets of the Lord. When he made his sensational entry into Jerusalem, we are told in the Matthaean account that the whole city was moved, as the people asked, 'Who is this?', to receive the answer, 'This is the prophet Jesus from Nazareth of Galilee' (Matt. 21:11). Evidence for this reaction is to be found at every stage of his ministry.

When the people thought of Jesus as a prophet, they were not thinking so much of the great succession of writing prophets from Amos to Malachi. Their minds turned to earlier and almost legendary figures, Elijah and Elisha. Elijah is the prophetic figure in the highest degree. He comes suddenly out of the desert; equally suddenly he disappears into the desert, and, as report had it, he is carried up in a whirlwind into heaven.

The strangeness of Elijah is, we might think, more akin to John the Baptist than to Jesus; indeed Jesus himself makes the identification in the solemn affirmation that Elijah has already come, and they have done to him whatever it was in their hearts to do (Mark 9:13). We might think the similarity to Jesus is to be found, rather, in the more peaceful and domestic prophet Elisha, to whom also is ascribed the performance of many miracles. Jesus touched the leper and healed him. But Elisha also had wrought the cure of the leper Naaman the Syrian, though to the annoyance of Naaman he avoided any direct contact with him (2 Kings 5:11). Elisha received a gift of twenty barley loaves from the unknown man of Baal-shalishah, and with this small supply fed a hundred men, so that they all ate, and some was left over. Jesus fed a multitude, with scanty provisions and, as in the story of Elisha, when all had eaten, a considerable supply of food was left over (2 Kings 4:42-44). Elisha raised from the dead the only son of a mother (2 Kings 4:6-37); Jesus raised from the dead the only son of a mother, and she a widow (Luke 7:11-17). When the records of the life of Jesus came to be written, such parallels could not escape the eyes of those who were familiar with the Old Testament; scholars have noted the deep impression, in style and structure, left by the stories of Elijah and Elisha on the Lucan narrative of the activities of Jesus.

But the performance of miracles, though an accompaniment of a prophetic ministry, was not an essential part of it. Nor was that feature, which has obscured for many readers the real nature of the prophetic office – the faculty of foretelling the future. It is true that the Old Testament prophets did foretell the future, often in terms of divine judgment on an ungrateful nation, but also in the form of such moving promises of restoration as are found in some of the later passages of the book of Jeremiah. Jesus also did on occasion foretell the future. Perhaps it did not demand a very great measure of intelligence to foresee the way in which events were tending among the Jews. The forces of discontent with the Roman domination were rising; strained nationalism and the expectation of divine help from heaven were captivating the minds of some; the rejection of Jesus himself could be taken as a portent of things to come. Jesus may have been more aware than many that futile resistance to the Roman power must lead to the destruction of the city and to the disintegration of the Jewish national existence. But through all such utterances runs a sublime sense of the authority and power of God, who holds all things in his hands, and works out his purposes through the tortuousness and self-deception of human wills not attuned to his.

We have not yet reached the heart of the prophetic consciousness, though we have evidences of it in what we have learned of the prophets of other nations. The prophet is one whose whole consciousness is filled with an overpowering sense of the nearness and reality of God; 'the Lord God has spoken; who can but prophesy?' (Amos 3:8).

The whole of this experience is presented in memorable language in no more than eight verses of the book of the Prophet Isaiah (6:1-8). Here it is all set out – a sense of the supreme and tremendous majesty of God; an awareness of the insignificance and infirmity of man: God's condescension in calling man to be his partner in the work that he has to do on earth; the free yet necessary obedience of the one who has heard the divine call. Jesus stands in the direct line of this prophetic experience. God has called him; God stands at the very centre and heart of his consciousness.

It was this quality of intimate fellowship with God at all times and in all places that first attracted the attention of the disciples. This is not to be described as familiarity – Jesus is the heir of that spirit of awe which fills all the Old Testament encounters with God. But this awareness of the unseen is not a matter of special times and places. He has such special times–

the Gospels are full of echoes of his need for prayer, of his escape from the crowded ways of men to be alone with the Father. But this awareness is something that is with him all the time. The most remarkable of all his recorded outbursts in prayer (Matt. 11:25-30) is introduced simply as the conclusion of a discourse on his predecessor and forerunner, John the Baptist.

Pious Jews were, of course, familiar with the great truth that God fills all things and that at any moment we may turn to him. But Judaism had to a large extent become a religion of exclusion. The temple in Jerusalem was still the centre of the religious life of the people, though no doubt there were many who had never seen it. But the way to the holiest was fenced by many barriers. Gentiles were rigorously excluded. We have the engraved notice which warns the incautious Gentile that, if he goes beyond this spot, he will be responsible for his own death – whether by the sudden stroke of God, or because any pious Jew, becoming aware of his intrusion, will have the right to kill him. Women could come only so far – in orthodox Jewish worship they are still segregated from the men. Lay male Israelites could penetrate further towards the sanctuary, but there was an enclosure reserved only for the priests, and into the holiest place of all only the high priest could enter once a year on the day of atonement. Jesus, like all good Jews, paid a due meed of respect to the temple, but he was singularly free from its limitations; God was the air he breathed, and he walked with supreme confidence in his Father's house.

If the prophet of Mecca could reply, in answer to a question, that his message dealt with God and with the day of judgment, Jesus might have answered that his message was like a single spear-thrust – it dealt with God, and with him only. Of course it does deal with many other things – in poems and parables and injunctions and prophecies. But at the heart and centre of all things is God. In the four Gospels there are no less than one hundred and seventy-five references to God as Father – the word which never once occurs in the Koran; it is God as my Father, as the Father, as your Father, one phrase following rapidly on another according to the context. To these must be added references to God, to the Lord, and so on. But clearly the aim of his teaching is to introduce his followers into the same intimacy with the Lord of heaven and earth as he felt himself to enjoy as Son.

It is perhaps not surprising that his hearers caught from him just this sense of access and intimacy. More surprising, perhaps, is the fact that they claimed to enjoy the reality not only when he was visibly with them, but when he was no more than an invisible presence. This continuing presence they had learnt from him to call the Spirit; this was the Spirit of Jesus, who came to complete and amplify that which they had learned through him. So it was almost a matter of indifference to them whether they spoke of Jesus with them, or the Spirit with them; in either case it was a continuous presence, the reality of which they had experienced when they had been with Jesus, and the reality of which was further attested to them by a wider range of experiences than those of Judaea and Galilee.

They made use of a number of different words and phrases to give expression to this wider range of experience. One of their favourite words was 'access' – that very thing which had been denied them under the Jewish system: 'through him we both have access in one Spirit to the Father,' writes St Paul (Eph. 2:18). This access is without fear, since it is to a Father whom Jesus has made known as the loving Father who is willing to receive all who turn to him with faith in Christ, through whom the barrier created by sin has finally been done away.

Even more striking is the language in which Paul speaks of those who have believed in Christ as having been raised to an entirely new level of existence in him and through him. God has raised Christ from the dead and caused him to sit down in the seat of majesty in the heavenly places, above all authority and power and dominion (Eph. 1:20-21). But Christ does not take his seat alone, he brings with him those whom God has raised up in his resurrection, to whom he has given new life and has given authority to take their place with him in the realms that are above the heavens (Eph. 1:20; 2:6).

That these are not just the isolated imaginings of one single writer is made clear by a number of passages in the Epistle to the Hebrews, the writer of which in a very different idiom makes a number of similar assertions. His thought moves in the area of the earthly tabernacle, in which God made known his presence to his people, but which is only a faint representation of the true sanctuary in the unseen world. Into the old earthly sanctuary Jesus would have had no right to enter, since he did not belong by birth to the priestly tribe. But now he has by death entered not into a sanctuary made by human hands, which cannot be more than a faint copy of the true sanctuary, but into heaven itself, there to appear in the presence of God on our behalf (Heb. 9:24). But here again he did not enter in alone; he has prepared for us also a new way through the veil which hides the sanctuary. That way is his body, offered for us in death but now raised from death by the power of God (Heb. 10:19-22). So, when we enter in, it is not into an earthly sanctuary, doomed to desolation and destruction, but into heaven itself, the true eternal indissoluble sanctuary. This is available to us now and not merely at the end of time.

One other quotation, from yet another writer of very different style and vision, will round off the series. The seer of the Revelation of St John has a vision of a rider on a white horse, whom the hosts of heaven follow; and on his robe and on his thigh he has a name written – King of kings and Lord of lords (Rev. 19:11,14,16).

It is worth recalling that some of these words were written probably not more than forty years after the death of the One about whom they were written, and at a time when a considerable number of people were still living who had seen and heard him. These are not the kind of words that we expect to be written by Jews who had been brought up to a rigid doctrine of monotheism; but Jewish they are in their thought and in their imagery. Moreover, even in what may appear the extravagance of their language, they never quite lose touch with that very human figure who meets us in the Gospels and who has become familiar to us as the prophet of Nazareth in Galilee.

No words like these have ever been written about the other

prophets who have come to our notice, or about others, such as Baha'ullah, the second founder of the Bahā'i movement (1817-92), of whose claim for himself we shall have to take note in another connection.

Zarathustra left to his people a number of poems and a set of principles, which have earned him the veneration of succeeding generations.

The Pali Canon of Buddhism records the great entrance of Gautama the Buddha into Nirvāna; in the less historical parts of the narrative, this great event is accompanied by signs and wonders in earth and heaven. But there is no suggestion that the Buddha will continue to be present with his followers after his death; the *dhamma*, the teaching, will take his place and will be their guide. His memory has been kept in the greatest reverence by those who have found in him the great Enlightener. Very soon after his death, the cult of the relics of the Buddha developed in the great *stūpas* in which these relics were preserved. But these were relics of a great man long since dead, and deservedly held in reverence among his faithful followers.[3]

The exact date of the death of the prophet Muhammad is known. No one has ever supposed that he survived the accident of physical death. Almost unlimited veneration has been accorded to him by his followers, and for this he has himself to be accounted in a measure responsible, in view of the exaggerated respect that he allowed to be paid to him by the faithful in his lifetime. But no one in the Islamic world has ever dreamed of according to him divine honours – he would have been the first to reject any such suggestion as blasphemy. In some of the traditions of Islam (sources secondary to the Koran and not of equal authority), it is sometimes hinted that on the day of judgment the Prophet will intervene as mediator,

3. I have here followed the Theravāda, or southern tradition of Buddhism. If account is taken of the Mahāyāna, or northern tradition, with its multiplicity of lords many and Buddhas many, the statement here made would have to be modified at a number of points.

and will save disciples in whose heart there is no more than a speck of goodness. But this is not borne out by the Koran itself. On that day, no mediation will be permitted; on that day none will avail.[4] The legacy of Muhammad is the Koran; that, as he believed, he has received from God and has faithfully handed on to man. It is for this that the gratitude of the believers is due to him. They will never mention his name without prayer for a blessing to him. But worship is to be addressed to God, and exclusively to him alone.

To return to Paul, the sum total of all that he ascribes to Jesus Christ can be summed up very simply in the words: 'that Christ may dwell in your hearts through faith; that you . . . may have power to comprehend with all the saints what is the breadth and length and height and depth, and to know the love of Christ which surpasses knowledge' (Eph. 3:17-19). Christ is that same Jesus who lived and died in the days of Pontius Pilate, but now is universally available through the Holy Spirit whom he promised to send in the Father's name, thus fulfilling universally the prophetic ministry which he began on earth.

Some of those who most deeply respect Jesus are of the opinion that his followers were mistaken in saying of him such things as have been recalled in this chapter. Such imaginings, they feel, come between Jesus and the reverent student, who wants to come as near to a human master as possible, and to know him as he was in his ways and works. They would like to put the Epistles on one side and to come back to the simplicities of the Gospel. They are entitled to their opinion, but there are certain difficulties in the way of following them. In the first place, the Gospels are not quite as simple as is often supposed; they stand at the end of a fairly long tradition of interpretation of the event of Christ, and, as the critical study of the Gospels has made plain in recent years, even the Gospel of Mark, which is accepted by many as the earliest of the Gospels, has a dense theological structure from which it is difficult to enucleate mere narrative. Secondly, the effect which Jesus had on those who

---

4. See Tor Andrae, *Mohammed: the Man and his Faith*, p.56.

believed in him is part of the story of Jesus, just as the accounts of the teaching of the Buddha in the traditions laid up by his disciples are part of the story of the Buddha.

The writers of the New Testament were not engaged in a process of mystification. They were trying to set down what Jesus had come to mean to them in the process of the days and the years. The New Testament owes its existence to many writers and to many editors, but there is an essential unity that runs through the whole; the aim of all the writers was that the memory of Jesus Christ should not perish from among the sons of men as long as the earth should last.

One aspect of the New Testament to which great attention has been paid by gifted scholars in recent years has been the development of worship in the early Christian fellowship of believers. Some great sections, notably the passage in Philippians 2 which describes the humiliation and the glory of Christ, have been identified as early Christian hymns, and are printed in this form in many modern translations of the Bible. Even in these early evidences, and still more in the great liturgies as they developed, we can trace a subtle blending of the past, the present, and the future.

There is constantly a reference to the historic event, to what actually took place, when Jesus the prophet from Nazareth in Galilee made among the people the great proclamation of the present and coming kingdom of God. As we know from the second-century writer, Justin Martyr, at least as early as his time the reading of the 'reminiscences of the apostles' formed part of regular Christian worship. But Jesus was not simply a voice from the past. When the believers met, probably in early days in very small groups, they were aware that Jesus was with them. The words that he himself was believed to have spoken, 'Where two or three are gathered together in my name, there am I in the midst of them', had been recorded in the Gospels. When they met together to remember him, they knew that it was so. They did not argue as to the nature of his presence; they did what he had ordained in the breaking of the bread, and the blessing of the cup – they knew that he was there.

But they knew that, though Jesus the prophet had

proclaimed the kingdom of God, that kingdom had now become a hidden kingdom. It had become like an underground river, the presence of which is at times startlingly shown in the fertility of fields that have been able to draw upon its waters. It is the task of the Church to set up signs of the kingdom, that its presence and its promise may never be forgotten. But Christians look forward with longing to the day when that kingdom is again proclaimed with power, and all the purposes of God in Christ are brought to their consummation.

To Christians, Christ is the king; the fulfilment of God's purposes is inseparably connected with the hope of his coming in glory. It is hard to put clear intellectual content into these words. We do not know what his coming will mean; we cannot even imagine a reality which is hidden from our senses as they now are. But Christians have never lost the confidence that their prophet will one day himself be the fulfilment of all that he foretold.

The New Testament closes with the words, 'He who bears witness to these things affirms: Of a truth I come suddenly', to which the Church joyfully replies: 'So be it; come, Lord Jesus' (Rev. 22:20 Gk).

A power from the unknown God
A Promethean conqueror came,
Like a triumphal path he trod
The thorns of death and shame.
A mortal shape to him
Was like the vapour dim
Which the orient planet animates with light;
Hell, sin and slavery came
Like bloodhounds mild and tame
Nor preyed until their Lord has taken flight.
The moon of Mahomet
Arose, and it shall set;
While, blazoned, as on heaven's eternal noon,
The Cross leads generations on.

P.B. Shelley, *Hellas.*

5

Jesus or Barabbas – which is the true Messiah?

Jesus said, 'Resist not evil.' Does this mean that the use of force is never acceptable?

The Old Testament is an open-ended book – it always looks towards a fulfilment beyond itself.

The thoughts of the people of Israel went back constantly to David their king, a David much idealised in memory, but still one who had lived, who had been appointed by God himself to be the true ruler of his people, one who more than any other had been the architect of the greatness of his people. David died and the people were laid low at the hands of their adversaries. But, strangely, past and future became confused in their minds, and the David who had been became the David who was to be, 'the once and future king'.[1]

'They shall be my people, and I will be their God. My servant David shall be king over them; and they shall all have one shepherd... David my servant shall be their prince for ever' (Ezek. 37:23-25). This future king will be free from the defects of his ancestors: 'Behold, a king will reign in righteousness, and princes will rule in justice. Each will be like a hiding place from the wind, a covert from the tempest, like streams of water in a dry place, like the shade of a great rock in a weary land' (Isa. 32:1-2). 'He shall not judge by what his eyes see, or decide

---

1. The title of the imaginative book about King Arthur by T.H. White.

by what his ears hear; but with righteousness he shall judge the poor, and decide with equity for the meek of the earth; and he shall smite the earth with the rod of his mouth, and with the breath of his lips he shall slay the wicked' (Isa. 11:3-4). It is hopes such as these that sustained the people of Israel in its darkest days; God has not forgotten his people, one day he will act on their behalf.

It is hard to say exactly what form these expectations for the future had taken in the minds of the Jews in the days when Jesus of Nazareth was among them. By taking every passage in the Old Testament which looks forward to the future, and by weaving them all together into a pattern, it is possible to arrive at a picture which can be made to resemble in many ways Jesus as we see him depicted in the Gospels. But this way of handling the material does not correspond closely with the situation as it really existed. Ordinary people did not have at hand, as we have, books containing the whole of the Old Testament revelation. What they had usually came to them in fragments, and largely by word of mouth. It is not surprising that there was a great variety of expectations, and that these were hard to reconcile with one another. Ideas of deliverance among the people were largely determined by that from which they felt that they needed to be delivered.

The people of Israel had become by conquest and against their will a part of the Roman Empire. In the western world the Romans had been extraordinarily successful rulers. After conquest had been firmly established, though resistance continued here and there the conquered peoples began to be proud of that greater unity into which they had been brought. They learnt Latin so successfully that some of the greatest writers in that language had not been born in Italy. As citizenship came to be extended, the proudest boast of all was to be able to say, 'I am a Roman citizen.'

Rome was far less successful among the eastern peoples, and least successful of all among the Jews. The Jewish people had had long and varied experience of being subjugated by conquerors. Their memories went back to the days of slavery in

Egypt. They had known Assyrians and Babylonians and Persians and Greeks. And the last, the Romans, were the worst of all because they were the most efficient. It was exasperating for the Romans to have to deal with a people that absolutely refused to be assimilated. Roman attitudes to religion were tolerant. Provided that people were prepared to acquiesce in the worship of the emperor, or more exactly of the 'genius' of the emperor, which was increasingly coming to be practised as the symbol of imperial unity, they could carry on as they liked with the worship of their own peculiar gods. The intransigent monotheism of the Jews was strange to the Roman mind; why could not this small Semitic people behave like everyone else?

Some among the Jews, like the family of the Herods, accepted the situation and made a good thing out of it. Many, no doubt, just got on with their own business, paid their taxes just about as resentfully as people always pay taxes, and otherwise kept out of politics. But there was a deep groundswell of anti-colonial bitterness, and a hope among the more pious Jews that the Roman domination might not last for ever. Inevitably, every resistance movement among the people raised the question whether this was the signal for the coming of Messiah, or at least a signal that the days of Messiah were about to begin.

The work of John the Baptist naturally raised considerable expectations – was this indeed the deliverer to whom the eager expectations of the people were looking forward? The ministry of Jesus in its early days, when it appeared primarily as a healing ministry, attracted widespread interest; the power of God was manifested in the overthrow of demons, and the messianic question could not but be raised. John's Gospel represents more than the others the kind of debates that were going on in Jerusalem. Some were saying, 'This is the Messiah', but others asked, 'Could the Messiah possibly come from half-pagan Galilee?' (7:40-43 Gk). The leaders expressed their resentment at the refusal of Jesus to declare himself, 'How long will you keep us in suspense? If you are the Messiah, tell us plainly and without evasion' (John 10:24 Gk).

Others in much more recent times have echoed this complaint. If he was the Messiah, why could he not say so, make his claims clear, and so help people to consider the claims and to decide whether to accept or to reject them? Adherents of the Bahā'i faith contrast the reticence of Jesus with the candour of Bahā'ullah, the second founder of their religion. When Bahā'ullah felt himself called of God to be the divine word to the nineteenth century, he wrote to the Pope and to Queen Victoria and to other potentates, informing them who he was, and urging them to admit that his claims were well founded and that his message was the truth.

There was, from the point of view of Jesus, very good reason for his refusal to define his claims until the very last moment of his ministry. His method was to speak and to show himself, but to let people discover for themselves who and what he was. Such a response alone would deserve the name of faith. Faith in Messiah, yes; but in what kind of a Messiah? It all depended on what kind of Messiah the people wanted, and the kind of Messiah that they were likely to accept. Some at least among the Jews wanted a heroic deliverer, a warrior like Judas Maccabaeus, who would raise the standard of revolt, smite down the Roman enemy, and set them free. To such the idea of a non-violent Messiah must have seemed much like a contradiction in terms. Evidence for the prevalence of this view of Messiah, among the common people, may perhaps be found in the episode of Barabbas to be found in the story of the death of Jesus. Nothing is known of this man apart from the allusion in the Gospels. He was, presumably, one of those zealots, whose activities kept the Roman authorities in Palestine in a state of constant apprehension, and whose abortive attempts to stir up insurrection against the overwhelming strength of the Romans led almost invariably to their capture and death. The name Barabbas, which means simply 'son of the father', tells us nothing special, though it has been held by some that the name implies that the insurrectionary was the son of a Rabbi. It is, however, interesting that in some manuscripts the personal name of Barabbas is given as Jesus. This reading was known to the great Alexandrian scholar Origen, but he rejected it, holding it unsuitable that a brigand should bear the same name as the Saviour of the world. If, however, the reading is correct, the contrast between the two becomes sensational. Here, on the one hand, is the 'Saviour' who has talked a great deal about the kingdom of God but has done nothing whatever to bring it in; on the other is the young man who, perhaps wrong-headedly, has at least struck a blow for freedom. When faced with such a contrast, there would be little reason to doubt the verdict of a crowd, already influenced by the propaganda of the enemies of Jesus – not this man but Barabbas. It is not difficult, in such a situation, to make it appear that violence is the better way. We know much less than we would like to know about the views of the Jews in the days of Jesus. But from the evidence that we have, it is clear that the idea of a violent Messiah was not far from the hopes and expectations of a not inconsiderable number among them. Gamaliel refers to one Theudas, who was slain and came to nothing; and also Judas the Galilean, who also perished and all who followed him were scattered (Acts 6:36-37). The tribune in charge of the arrest of Paul imagined him to be the Egyptian, who 'stirred up a revolt and led the four thousand men of the Assassins out into the wilderness.' (Acts 21:38). We know little of these shadowy figures; as a result of archaeological discoveries we now know far more than was known until very recent times of the final explosion that took place just a century after the time of Jesus.

The destruction of Jerusalem by the Romans in AD 70 was a tremendous disaster; yet it became clear that the vengeful spirit of the Jews had not been crushed even by that vast calamity. The rebellion of the year AD 131 was, in the opinion of a great authority (Schürer) 'an uprising that in scope, dynamic power and destructive consequences was at least as violent as that of the days of Vespasian.'

The name of the leader of the insurrection was Simon. His official title was 'Prince of Israel', but he was commonly known as Bar-Kocheba, 'Son of the Star', an allusion to the Star which should arise out of Jacob (Num. 24:17) – a clear indication that he claimed to be, and was regarded by his followers as being, the Messiah, the anointed of God.

The rebellion spread far and wide, and with it the hope that the kingdom of God had at last come. From the desert of Judaea coins have been recovered bearing the inscription 'for the freedom of Israel', or 'Year I of the liberation of Israel', or 'Year II of the freedom of Israel' – reminiscent of the language of the French revolution. But as before the Jews had greatly underestimated the power and the persistence of Rome. In the year AD 135 the last stronghold of the rebels was captured and the uprising came to an end. Jerusalem was given the new name *Aelia Capitolina*, and turned into an entirely pagan city. The Jews had access to it only once in the year, on the anniversary of the destruction of Jerusalem, to make their lamentation, at the Wall of Wailing, for all that they had lost. All this Jesus had clearly foreseen.

Those who lived in India through the years in which the independence of India was being worked out were faced by a tragically similar confrontation. One of the more ardent supporters of the movement for the emancipation of India judged that political assassination was an acceptable mode of procedure, was apprehended and sentenced to death. There was a practical clash between the teachings of the Mahātmā, who was urging his people to accept the principles of *satyāgraha*, spiritual action, and *ahimsā*, the rejection of violence, and the veneration accorded in considerable sections of the population to one who was regarded as a martyr in the cause of freedom.

Violence or non-violence? This was precisely the dilemma which faced Mohandas Karamchand Gandhi, when in 1915, after his successful career in South Africa, he returned to India. By that time, the nationalist movement in India had split into divergent, and at times mutually hostile, streams. On the one hand were the Indian liberals, committed to non-violence and to constitutional advance; on the other was the revolutionary wing, headed, until his death in 1920, by Bal Gangadhar Tilak, who was prepared to defend assassination in the cause of freedom, and later by Subhas Chandra Bose, who became for a short time President of Congress in 1939, and in 1943 declared war on Britain and the United States in the name of a free India. Which was Gandhi to choose? The veteran Gopal Krishna Gokhale spent hours with him trying to persuade him to join the peaceful wing. It is strange that the apostle of non-violence threw in his lot with the violent, hoping no doubt to persuade them to adopt his special version of the creed of non-violence.

Like Gandhi, Jesus had to choose. Was he a totally committed votary of non-violence? Some critics have doubted his right to this claim; it is only fair to give a little space to the consideration of the arguments they adduce in support of their case.

Jesus cursed a fig-tree, and it withered away (Mark 11:12-14, 21-24). Does not this indicate an outburst of what the Indian Professor Radhakrishnan calls 'nervous irritation'? It is by no means clear that this is the case. In Luke's Gospel, Jesus is reported as having uttered a parable about a fig-tree which bore no fruit (Luke 13:6ff). (Some scholars hold that this is the original account, and that Matthew and Mark have turned what was a story into an incident.) Clearly the fig-tree in the parable is a picture of Israel, the people to whom God came looking for the fruits of righteousness and failing to find them; a further stay of judgment will be permitted, but this will be the last. In the incident as recorded by Matthew and Mark, the symbolic character of the words of Jesus is no less unmistakable. Everyone in Palestine knew that on the fig-tree the fruit is formed before the leaves; anyone, therefore, seeing the tree in leaf, would be entitled to expect that the fruit would have already been formed. Was Israel indeed a people of God? If, beneath the outward show of temple worship, there was no inner reality, might it not be concluded that the day of judgment had already come? The words of Jesus indicate not so much anger as sorrowful recognition that the hopes that God has set on Israel had not been fulfilled.

Some, absurdly, have interpreted the cleansing of the temple as an act of violence on the part of Jesus. How could one single man impose his will by violence on a crowd? Undoubtedly the prophetic authority with which Jesus stood before them, and the words, more sorrowful than scornful, in which he condemns their presence in the temple, impressed upon them a sense of guilt and fear which excluded the possibility of resistance. Certainly the whip of small cords, which he made, was a symbol of authority. But, as the New Testament scholar Edwyn Hoskyns, always a countryman at heart, remarked, 'If you are going to drive cattle and sheep, it is rather useful to have something to drive them with.' The whip and the animals are mentioned only in the fourth Gospel, and there is no suggestion in any of the four Gospels that Jesus so much as touched any single human being.

A much more difficult passage is that in Luke's Gospel, where Jesus is represented as saying, 'let him who has no sword sell his mantle and buy one'; to which the disciples reply, 'Lord, here are two swords', and his answer is, 'It is enough' (Luke 22:36–38). This seems to run counter to the warning recorded in the same context in Matthew: 'all who take the sword will perish by the sword' (Matt. 26:52). It may be, however, that the explanation is so simple as often to have passed unnoticed. The last days of the life of Jesus must have been for him, as for the disciples, a time of immense emotional strain. The Lord was human; it would be strange if the inner conflict left no trace on his outward manner and his speech. There is, in point of fact, just the kind of evidence we might have expected. His utterances take on a note of irony such as is not to be found in the earlier days of the ministry. When he comes to the disciples the third time in the garden of Gethsemane and finds them sleeping, he says to them, 'Are you still sleeping and taking your rest?' (Mark 14:41) – a fine time to be sleeping, when he who betrays me is already close at hand. So also, in the passage about the swords, the meaning may surely be, 'A fine time this to be thinking of human measures of resistance, when our little band can hardly expect to be able to stand against the forces that are massing against us.' And, when the disciples, who have been doing exactly that, taking thought for resistance, naïvely answer, 'Here are two swords', his words 'that is enough' may be taken not as meaning 'two will be sufficient' but rather as 'that is the last straw'.[2] Even now they have understood so little of his teaching and of his intentions.

As against these few passages the main lines of the teaching of Jesus are perfectly clear. He lays stress on the avoidance of violence, on patient endurance of wrongs done to us, and abandonment of any right to retaliate. The principle is clearly laid down; when it comes to the application of the principle, difficulties may present themselves and differences of opinion may arise even among those who are prepared to take the Lord's words seriously.

One of the figures of speech that is most common in the words of Jesus is hyperbole, exaggeration, putting the extreme case. When Peter asks whether he should forgive his brother up to seven times, Jesus answers, 'I do not say to you seven times, but seventy times seven' (Matt. 18:22). I remember to have read in early years a charming story about a younger brother and sister who were much afflicted by the attentions of an aggressive older brother. Having read the verse in the Gospel, they decided to enter all his offences in a book and number them; up to the four hundred and ninetieth they must be willing to endure – but with the four hundred and ninety-first the right to retaliation will dawn! Such are the perils of literal interpretation of figures of speech; older readers are not likely to doubt that what Jesus is prescribing is unlimited endurance of the wrongs that are done against us.

The most famous utterance of all is, of course, 'I say to you, do not resist one who is evil. But if any one strikes you on the right cheek, turn to him the other also' (Matt. 5:39). Once again the principle is clear. We are not to claim any rights for ourselves. Everyone else has rights; we have only duties.

---

2. Of recent commentators, I.H. Marshall and E.E. Ellis both accept this interpretation.

Whether it is ever justifiable to use violence in defence of the rights of others is, perhaps, the most perplexing of all the questions that arise out of the text of the Gospels.

For the first three centuries of its existence, the Church on the whole remained faithful to the teaching of its Master. In part this arose out of conviction; in part it was due to the simple fact that the Church, as a threatened and persecuted minority, could not do otherwise. In times of persecution, some excited Christians acted provocatively and brought about their own deaths; but the Church wisely ruled that such were not to be enrolled as among the noble army of martyrs. When Constantine made Christianity the accepted religion of the empire, the situation was entirely changed, and, in the opinion of many, permanently changed for the worse.

Constantine himself was not a persecutor. But, before the end of the fourth century, Theodosius (379-395) had introduced enactments which told heavily against the interests of those who would not accept the Christian faith.[3] In the sixth century, the orthodox emperor Justinian turned his arms against the simpler peoples in remote areas of Asia Minor and elsewhere which had continued to resist the appeal of the Gospel. When Charlemagne defeated the Saxons in war, he offered them peace only on condition that they accepted baptism and submitted themselves to the law of Christ. So the long tale of woe continues through the centuries. Christians have complained of the tactics of the Muslims, with their idea of the holy war against unbelievers; history suggests that the balance of violence may not have been always on the side of the Muslims. The difference remains, however, that Christians have carried out holy wars in defiance of their Master, whereas the Muslim has in the Koran, in the traditions and in the law books, adequate support for the view that the carrying on of

---

3. 'This intention was implemented in a series of revolutionary measures, by virtue of which the accumulated debris of centuries was contemptuously swept away.' C.N. Cochrane, *Christianity and Classical Culture*, p.329.

war against the unbelievers, unless and until they are converted to Islam, is a sacred duty.

It is unlikely that any Christian today would defend methods which, in the past, were regarded as acceptable by many Christians. We have come to see that the decision to follow Christ must be a matter of free choice and of nothing else; any kind of coercion is excluded. But this does not immediately solve all problems relating to the application in all circumstances of Christ's rule of non-violence. The sharp division of opinion among devout Christians is evident to any intelligent observer today.

Some will take the line of a radical simplification of the problem. Violence is always evil. Evil is always to be avoided. Therefore in no circumstances can a Christian become involved in the use of violence.

This simplistic solution overlooks the fact that only rarely in life are we faced by a clear and direct choice between good and evil. Much more often our choices must be between two possible goods, or between two forms of evil.

A girl feels a very strong conviction that she ought to go abroad on missionary service. But she has an ailing mother, who is deeply dependent on the help that she can give better than anyone else. To become a missionary is a good thing. To care for a dependent mother is also a good thing. How is it possible to decide which is the greater good? There is no strictly rational method of calculation; nor can anyone decide for another what is the right decision in such circumstances. All that can be done is to weigh up all the factors in the situation as objectively as possible, to ask for the guidance of God, and then decide, in the hope that through the consequences it will become evident that the choice was right. Christians are not endowed with the gift of infallibility.

War is always evil. But are there evils greater even than war? To this question some Christians will give emphatically the answer that no evil can be greater than war; for them it is clear that to be a Christian is also to be a pacifist. To others the answer is by no means so clear.

Almost all Christians of my age, in Britain and probably elsewhere, tended towards pacifism between the two world wars. We had seen the fearful destruction wrought by the first great war; the generation just before our own had been almost wiped out, and this loss had left leadership in the country gravely and perhaps permanently impoverished. We were inclined to say, 'Never again.' But then the world gradually became aware of what Hitler was doing in Germany. Can we accept responsibility for allowing this to go on? We ought not to resist wrongs done to ourselves; but have we the right to make unwilling martyrs of others whom it might be possible for us to defend? In March 1939 Hitler, unprovoked, marched into Prague, shot up a number of Czech students and imprisoned the Czech professors. At that moment many of us reached the point of saying, 'This man must be stopped, at literally any cost.' It was an agonising decision; in the light of all that has happened since, it is hard to say whether it was the right decision or not; if Hitler could be stopped only at the price of unleashing Stalin, did the world gain or lose by the operation?

Christians in Germany had to face the same issue in an even more perplexing way. Should Hitler be allowed to continue? Or are there situations in which the extreme exercise of tyranny make it permissible to say that 'killing is no murder'? In 1944 a plot to assassinate Hitler was formed, and was very nearly successful. A number of those involved in the plot were sincere and devout Christians. Among the conspirators, the best-known in England and America was Dietrich Bonhoeffer. The steps by which he was led to the decision to take part have been well documented, and make plain the agonies through which he passed. To Bonhoeffer it was clear that to take part in a conspiracy to murder is sin. It is not enough to say that sin can be forgiven. Forgiveness may be asked, but only if there is a sincere conviction that the sin has been committed in order to avoid the commission of a greater sin. Just before the end of the war, Bonhoeffer was hanged by the Nazis for his complicity in the conspiracy. In Britain and America he is very widely honoured as a martyr; this is a verdict in which many Christians in Germany do not concur; to them the martyrs are the many who died unresisting in Hitler's concentration camps for no other crime than that of refusing to go along with that which they saw to be wrong.

The same questions are being raised today, and are proving as perplexing and as divisive as they were forty and fifty years ago. In 1982 the general sentiment in Britain and the United States was that the illegal occupation of the Falkland Islands by the Argentinians must be resisted by force. Dissentients were comparatively few. In many parts of the world, the peoples groan and suffer under oppressive governments. Supporters of 'liberation theology', especially in Latin America, are convinced that there is no way out of this situation other than by revolution; gradual and constitutional change is a remedy that is no longer adequate or acceptable. But revolution almost always involves violence. Can Christians accept the evils of violence as the only way to the avoidance of the greater evils of oppression and injustice?

Is there any case, then, for believing that Jesus is the true victor, that he is the prince of peace and that his way is the only way in which God's will can be done on earth?

Through the centuries it is the crucified Christ who has drawn the hearts of men and women to himself. Cross and resurrection must be held together as they always are in the New Testament. But it is the sheer helplessness of the Man of Calvary, and his absolute trust that God will bring victory out of defeat, life out of death, that has given countless believers the courage to attempt the impossible and to give up life itself for the sake of the truth. There is in existence a strange reading in some Greek manuscripts of the 96th Psalm: 'tell it out among the nations that the Lord hath reigned from the tree'. This is certainly not what the Psalmist wrote, but it is equally certainly the message that the Scriptures convey, and what the voice of history has declared to be true. It is said that Mahatma Gandhi had a picture of the crucifixion in his own working study and that his favourite hymn was, 'When I survey the wondrous cross'.

But the way of non-violence is not an easy way out. The Bible does not suggest that peace, in the sense of the cessation of war, is necessarily a good thing in itself. What we are told is that the effect of *righteousness* will be peace (Isa. 32:17), and that only by seeking righteousness can we really try to establish peace. The *Shalom* of the Scriptures is that which comes about when the will of God is fully and perfectly done.

The Christian, therefore, must be fully and whole-heartedly committed to the cause of justice in the world. But this is far easier to say than to make effective. Even with the help of the best sources that we have available, it is in many cases almost impossible to determine what are the rights and wrongs in any particular case. Again and again the Christian is tempted to say, as countless Christians said at the time of the Spanish civil war, 'A plague on both your houses'. The victory of either side seemed bound to lead only to dissension and to oppression. But we must not give up the struggle. We are called to know, to pray, and to serve as far as we are able, when we see wrong and injustice to call them by their proper names, not to withdraw from the struggle into the euphoria of inner contemplation but to be there, at least in spirit, where the principles of Jesus are denied and his law is disobeyed.

The way of peace was for him the way of suffering. It is certain to be so for those who accept him as the true victor and pledge themselves to his service.

> *It may be that there is a higher wisdom than ours, a more profound logic than any constructed by the human mind, in the light of which love and its attendant sacrifices could be proved to be the only truly rational law of life. But, if we are to talk of wisdom and logic as we know them, if we ask what rational human judgment has to say, then the verdict will always be the same. Throughout their history men have approved of love; they have never approved of making love absolute. And that the all-good, who is also the all-powerful, should renounce the exercise of power and allow goodness to be ground under the heel of evil may be magnificent – but*

it revolts our commonsense. At the end of the most fundamental and significant of all its quests the wisdom of man finds itself face to face with the foolishness of God.

J.A. Baker, *The Foolishness of God* (1975[2]), pp. 142-3.

6

The one Son, through whom all can become sons

'All men are brothers.' Is this obviously true, or does it become true only through the Son, who taught us to address God as our Father?

'We do not stone you for a good work but for blasphemy, because you being a man make yourself out to be God' (John 10:33 Gk).

This is for Jews and Muslims and for many perplexed devout Christians the chief stumbling block. How can God have a Son? Or how can a man climb up to be God?

It is well known that the Prophet Muhammad bitterly and contemptuously rejected the idea that Jesus could be the Son of God. He had received some information about Christianity at various stages of his career; but he seems not to have become acquainted with this central Christian doctrine until well on in his ministry in Mecca, and perhaps only shortly before he moved to Medina (AD 622). In one of the earliest Suras, cxii, the Prophet declares the unity of God: 'Say, God is one God; the eternal God, he begetteth not, neither is he begotten; and there is not anyone like unto him.' This seems to be a general declaration against polytheism, and to have no specific Christian reference. Much more explicitly in Sura xix, entitled 'Mary', is it declared that God cannot have a Son: 'This was Jesus the son of Mary: the Word of truth concerning whom they doubt. It is not meet for God that he should have any son: God forbid! When he decreeth a thing, he only saith unto it, Be;

and it is. And verily God is my Lord and your Lord: wherefore, serve him; this is the right way.'

Muhammad, apparently, never had any understanding of the sense in which Christians use the word 'Son'; he seems to have understood it in a way that would involve physical connotations, and this he naturally and rightly repudiated. He seems, indeed, to have supposed the Trinity as understood by Christians to be made up of God, Jesus and the Virgin Mary; there is, at least, no evidence that the Christian doctrine of the Trinity was ever explained to him. The Jews affirm the absolute unity of God: 'Hear, O Israel: the Lord our God is one Lord.' (Deut. 6:4). Some Jews, in the time of Muhammad, perhaps understood the Christian doctrine of the incarnation as expressing belief in a man Jesus, who somehow or another climbed up to be God. Some Christians undoubtedly have held a view similar to this; it may have been the heresy, technically called Adoptionism, that Muhammad encountered and condemned. It is possible that he neither knew nor condemned the faith by which the Church has lived through the centuries.

If we start from the Old Testament, we may find an approach to the problem less perplexing than that of resolute and absolute denial.

The term 'Son of God' is used in the Hebrew scriptures in several connections as implying a specially close relationship to God, a special dependence on him. In the great hymn of creation in the book of Job, angels are called the sons of God: 'When the morning stars sang together, and all the sons of God shouted for joy' (Job 38:7). Israel as a nation is called the son of God: 'When Israel was a child, I loved him, and out of Egypt I called my son.' (Hos. 11:1). Of the promised king of Israel, whose royal throne is to be established for ever, God declares that, 'I will be his father, and he shall be my son' (2 Sam. 7:14). Again, in a specially messianic passage, it is written of God: 'You are my son,' he said; 'this day I become your father' (Ps. 2:7 NEB). All these passages together do not amount to an explanation of what the New Testament writers mean when they refer to Jesus as the Son of God; they may, however, afford some clue as to the direction in which we may look for the explanation.

The Old Testament background is always important for the understanding of Jesus. But this is not the only direction in which we may look for an understanding of fatherhood and sonship. Some who object to religion, and in particular to the Christian revelation, do so on the ground that Christians are always looking for a father figure, and that this stigmatises them as unwilling to grow up and to accept reality, unable to face the demands of freedom, and always clinging to an imaginary support which will protect them from the burden of adult responsibility. There may be Christians to whom their faith is a refuge from reality and responsibility. If so, their attitude is due to a misunderstanding and not to an acceptance of the teaching of the New Testament. In that source of revelation, there is repeated emphasis on maturity. In a number of the English versions, this is obscured by the translation 'perfect' or 'perfection', which in many contexts may be more suitably translated 'maturity'. Thus when Paul says that he makes it his aim to 'present every man perfect in Christ' (Col. 1:28), a more exact rendering would be 'mature, full-grown, fully adult in Christ'. Many fathers delight in the company of little children. But almost all take pleasure in watching the growth of sons from childhood to manhood; some think of the son as the one who will succeed them in the business that they have built up, and will take over the direction when they themselves are not able to exercise it. That this is so in many cases is a simple fact of observation.[1]

Jesus was reputed to be the son of a carpenter. This means that he grew up in the world of intelligent and independent artisans, in which a craft is handed on in a family from one generation to another in unbroken succession. This world, with which Karl Marx seems not to have been well acquainted,

1. One friend of mine in the publishing business is a member of the sixth generation of those who have been members of the firm no less than of the family.

has not completely disappeared in England even today. The ancient village crafts of the hedger, the ditcher and the thatcher can still sometimes be found; they can hardly be learned otherwise than in the father-son relationship. In India, where in the villages the caste system maintains its almost unbroken sway, the traditional family can still be found in undisturbed perfection.

If you are a carpenter, it can be taken for granted that your father was a carpenter and your grandfather was a carpenter; it can equally be taken for granted that your son will grow up as a carpenter, and if, as a good Hindu, you live to see the face of your grandson, you will see one who is predestined also to be a carpenter. The mysteries of the trade are handed on from generation to generation, and each family is likely to have some special skills, or a special knack of carrying out the jobs that have to be done.

The stages in a boy's career are quite clearly marked. As soon as he begins to be able to work, that is to say at about the age of five or six, with schooling as an interlude or an interruption, he stands by his father, watching; it may be his proud privilege to hold the needed tools and to hand them to his father as they are required. All the time he is absorbing, almost without knowing it, the rudiments of the craft. By the time that he is thirteen or fourteen, he is able to carry out on his own a number of the simpler jobs; but the wise father is always in the background to make sure that the job is carried out with the requisite precision and address, or to help the boy if the job that he has been given proves to be rather too exacting for the level of skill that he has attained. By the time that the son has reached the age of nineteen or twenty, he should have attained to the full understanding of all the secrets of the craft; the father has taught him all that he himself knows, and, though both may be illiterate, there is a vast amount of traditional knowledge that has been shared, and a sense of beauty, proportion and fitness which is absorbed rather than systematically worked out or intellectually analysed.

So now there comes about the period of intelligent co-operation. The father still maintains the general direction of the work; but, when a contract has been entered into, the son is left on his own to see to the carrying out of the work, though always with the right to consult the father; and sometimes even to insist on his own way, if new tools appear to be better adapted than the old to meet the demands of changing situations. (Our ideal picture does not rule out the possibility that younger sons may break out from the parental world, judging their own abilities in the light of growing opportunities.) As years pass, the time will come when the father feels the need of rest, and is content to hand on responsibility for the family fortunes to the one who has now proved himself fully capable of assuming the responsibility, and who, if he is so fortunate, has standing by him a grown-up son who, in his turn, will be able to bear his full share of the weight of labour and concern.

In the world in which Jesus grew up, and especially, perhaps, in the Jewish world with its intense tradition of family loyalty and family continuity, these three stages of obedience, understanding and intelligent co-operation were clearly marked and have left their impress on the understanding of fatherhood and sonship as these are expressed in the pages of the New Testament.

Societies in the Middle East were slave-owning societies. Slavery, well established in the Old Testament though mitigated by humanitarian feelings and regulations, had died out in Israel by the time of Jesus. But the system, with all its accompanying abominations, was well known to every Jew, and especially to those who lived in the great cities of the Roman Empire, and saw the system in operation all around them. The contrast between the slave and the son runs right through the New Testament.

The contrast was painful and evident. In some of the slave-owning societies of the first century AD, slaves may actually have outnumbered free citizens. Slaves were not invariably badly treated. They were a valuable form of property, and wise masters saw to it that they were reasonably well treated and contented. In those hard days, when captives in war were almost certain to be enslaved, the slave might be better educated than his master, and could become a valued and useful member of the family; it might even be possible for him to earn enough to ransom himself and recover his freedom; the 'freedmen' were a well-known class in Roman society, and some of them attained to positions of considerable eminence in the state. But for many the gap between slave and free was always there – the slave had no rights, and was wholly dependent on the will of his master. Euripides in the fifth century BC told the truth when he said that slavery takes away from a man half his manhood. Tacitus records that in the reign of Nero, the senate in Rome condemned to death all the slaves of a city prefect who had been murdered by one of them.[2]

So Jesus in the fourth Gospel has profound things to say about slavery and freedom. 'A slave does not know what his master is doing' (John 15:15 Gk). This was literally true in many slave-owning societies; the slave was kept just at the menial jobs; he would pick up a good deal of knowledge as he went along, but the secrets of the trade were not revealed to him, being kept solely as the privilege of the family. In Georgia, during the days of slavery, it was strictly forbidden to teach a slave to read – once knowledge was within reach of the slave, it was also within his power to acquire a new sort of manhood, and to bridge at least in a measure the gap which divided him from the members of the family.

Moreover, continues Jesus, the slave has no permanent right of membership in the household; the position of the son is permanent and unchangeable (John 8:35). This was the terrible fact. Over the head of the slave hung the possibility that he might be sold down the river and lose the fellowship of family and friends. Cohabitation was permitted to slaves; regular and permanent marriage was not. So, in the strictest sense of the

---

2. *Annals* XIV, 42-5. But Tacitus also records that many were found to disapprove of what appeared to them to be a barbarous decision.

words, 'If the Son makes you free, you will be free indeed' (John 8:36).

All these ideas came together in the New Testament ideas of sonship. And Jesus set himself to work out for our sakes the New Testament pattern of obedience, understanding and intelligent co-operation.

The Epistle to the Hebrews tells us (5:8) that, 'Although he was a Son, he learned obedience through what he suffered.' This Epistle, a strange waif among the New Testament letters, opens with one of the most splendid eulogies of the greatness of Christ as the Son, and perhaps for that reason, almost more than any other New Testament text, speaks relentlessly about what it meant to live as the Son of God among men. We learn by experience, and, because we live in a world of clashing and imperious wills, including our own, that experience is bound to have in it an element of suffering. So it was with him. The picture presented to us in the Gospels is of one who lived without any protection or privilege, unsheltered and exposed to all the roughness of life in a Syrian country town. He, too, had to learn what it meant to pick and choose his path among tortuous ways, to distinguish unerringly the way of God's will from the way of self-pleasing.

It is a mistake to dwell too much on the sufferings of Christ – the Gospels themselves are astonishingly laconic in what they write; after all, in those days everyone knew what crucifixion was like, and there was no need to describe it in detail. Christ's sacrifice was what it was only as the climax of a life lived, to the fullest point of human development, in one continuous act of obedience. Each day brings to us its variety of temptations; it cannot have been otherwise with him, though the temptations he had to face were almost certainly other, and much subtler, than those we are called on to encounter. Just as the muscles grow by daily exercise, so his will through the years became tempered steel to face the final testing and to emerge from the testing as victor: 'I come to do thy will, O God.' In the final act of surrender, obedience had its perfect work.

Theologians have debated endlessly the problem of the

special knowledge which Jesus may have possessed as Son of God. What is clear from the Gospel narratives is that the knowledge which came to Jesus, whatever its special depth and clarity, must have come to him through the operations of a human brain and a human intelligence. Even the critics of Jesus, and these are many, are likely to admit that he had a remarkable faculty of observation, a keen understanding of men and of their minds, a well-disciplined faculty of weighing up a variety of situations and of assessing the exact weight to be assigned to each of the factors involved. Moreover, he must have been aware that he had unusual gifts as a leader of those whom he called to follow him.

By ceaseless acts of self-discipline, the will of Jesus was set at all times to do the will of God. It does not follow that it was at every moment transparently clear what that will of God must be. We are familiar with the problem; we may infer that, allowing for the difference between his vocation and ours, the problems that he had to face were much the same as those with which we are familiar.

On this point we are not left without evidence; the brilliant story of the temptations in the wilderness may be our guide. This must have come from Jesus himself – there was no one else there. We find here, as in so many of his sayings, a vivid faculty of imagination, and an almost mordantly exact realisation of the way things are. These are all 'kingdom' temptations. Jesus is aware both of his vocation and his capacity to fulfil it – the tremendous experience of the baptism has given him assurance of both. What kind of a kingdom is it that he is going to proclaim and to introduce?

In the first place, it is not to be a welfare state, in which the provision for elementary human needs is to be the first consideration. Both parts of the reply of Jesus to the tempter are to be noted. Marxists and liberals alike have been so concerned to supply bread for men's mouths that they have been tempted to overlook the relevance of the spiritual, of the word that comes from the mouth of God. The churches have been tempted so to concentrate on the spiritual side of their operations as to forget that physical hunger and thirst exercise a clamant demand to be satisfied. General William Booth said truly that it is not possible to preach the Gospel to men with empty stomachs. His solution was both to open soup kitchens in the East End of London, and also to proclaim a Gospel of the love of God that he believed sinners would hear and understand. Whenever the Church has been true to its founder, it has found itself constrained to provide a Gospel for the whole man.

The temptation to leap from the pinnacle of the temple has often been misunderstood. There is no reference to the crowds standing in the temple courts and being dazzled by an astonishing miracle of preservation. The point is to be sought elsewhere; the clue is in the reference to the angels which will be on guard to hold up the reckless leaper. Jesus is here rejecting any right to special protection and privilege to which, in view of the immense importance of his vocation, he might have been tempted to lay claim. The servant of the kingdom is not to embark on forlorn hopes, to risk his life recklessly when nothing useful can come from the adventure. A man set out single-handed to climb Mount Everest, believing that nothing was needed other than a resolute will. Naturally the next expedition found his dead body half-way up the mountain. A pious Christian set out to convert Nigeria, with no knowledge of a language and no provision for his needs; naturally within a very short time he was found dead in the Nigerian forest. The Lord is glorified in the devotion of his children, but not in the reckless folly which squanders life when it ought to be preserved.

The third temptation relates to the means by which the kingdom is to be brought in. Most kingdoms have been won by an adroit combination of force and fraud, the devil's weapons. The use of any such weapons in the service of the kingdom of God will clearly be self-defeating. The weapons of Satan will be effective only in bringing in the kingdom of Satan. The kingdom of God needs other servants: 'He will not wrangle or cry aloud, nor will any one hear his voice in the streets; he will not break a bruised reed or quench a smouldering wick' – but for all that he will bring 'justice to victory; and in his name will the Gentiles hope' (Matt.12:19–21, quoting Isa. 42:2,3,4).

Our wills should always point like a compass to the will of God – in point of fact, all the time they are in danger of being diverted by other things that have no business to be there. There is a heartbreaking story of Joseph Conrad about a ship's captain who ran his ship on the rocks, unaware that a jealous colleague had placed enough scrap iron in the neighbourhood of the compass to make certain that it would be unreliable and would lead the ship to disaster. In one way or another most of us have had similar experiences.

The will of God always has to do with a 'what' and a 'when'; knowing the 'what' and the 'when' is an essential requirement for co-operating with it.

Jesus, in the fulfilment of his ministry, found it necessary to spend long periods, sometimes whole nights, in prayer. Little is recorded of the contents of these; it is a fairly safe inference that the main concern of them, to keep up our metaphor, was precisely maintaining the compass inflexibly in its direction of true north. One rather clear hint of this is given in the note that, before the choice of the twelve disciples, Jesus spent the night in prayer. It was clear to him that the time had come for him to select an élite from among his followers, on whom the success and the continuity of his mission would largely depend. The number twelve, reminiscent of the twelve fathers of the tribes of Israel, gives a special solemnity to the occasion. So much depends on the right choice being made. Simon, son of Jonah, has it in him to become a rock, but there is also too much friable stone about him. The sons of thunder are temperamental and ambitious, but perhaps they have in them the capacity to grow. And Judas? What is to be made of Judas, the cleverest of the lot and probably the most ambitious? Yes, he must be given his chance – a chance that is to be renewed again and again until the last possible moment.

What in the world was it that led Judas to betray his friend? It has been plausibly suggested that his mistake was not in the 'what?' but in the 'when?'. It may have seemed to him that Jesus was delaying too long in declaring himself. Let him be delivered into the hands of his enemies, and then surely he must call upon God to deliver him from the hands of those enemies, and to show himself to be on the side of the one who is now to be revealed as the true Messiah. Only when it is too late does Judas realise that it is he who has miscalculated – there is to be no deliverance. And so he takes what seems to him to be the only way out for one burdened with so intolerable a load of guilt.

Cut is the branch that might have grown full straight,
And burned is Apollo's laurel bough.
(Marlowe, *Dr Faustus.)*

In the fourth Gospel, the inner conflicts of Jesus find expression in the formula, 'his hour was not yet come'. There is a *kairos*, an appointed moment, in the affairs of men. If God's will is to be done, it must be done when it should be done, and not at any other time. The reference may be to some comparatively insignificant event, such as renewing the supply of wine which had fallen short at a marriage feast. Or it may be in relation to an event of supreme importance.

The problem of Gethsemane may have been a problem of *kairos* more than of anything else. Has the moment come at which the issue of the kingdom of God and the kingdom of man must be played out to its final determination? Are the law-courts of Jews and Herodians and Romans to be given one final chance to do justice and to prove worthy of themselves? Are the common people to be given one final chance to recognise their king, and to choose Jesus and not Barabbas? Are the disciples to be given a chance to show their mettle, to respond as they should to the challenge of danger? Or has the moment not yet come? The faith of the disciples is still so weak. If they should fail? Do they not need further training in the way? It would be so easy to escape while the going is good, to find refuge with the loving friends in Bethany, to hide in the parts round Caesarea Philippi, or perhaps even to seek an easier ministry among the Gentiles. And the answer comes, 'This is their hour'; no further delay is possible, the enemy is already on the march, and the voice of the betrayer is heard in the garden.

The fourth Gospel is, to a large extent, a meditation on 'intelligent co-operation with God'. Jesus is aware that he comes from God, and speaks only the things that he has heard with the Father: 'I have not spoken on my own authority; the Father who sent me has himself given me commandment what to say and what to speak' (12:49), 'I am not alone, for the Father is with me' (16:32). 'I and the Father are one' (10:30; the meaning is 'one in will and in purpose'). When Philip requests him, 'Lord, show us the Father, and we shall be satisfied,' Jesus replies, 'Have I been with you so long, and yet you do not know me, Philip? He who has seen me has seen the Father' (14:8-9). It is unlikely that, at the time, they realised what Jesus meant, but in course of time they realised the meaning; they found that, whenever they thought of God, they thought of Jesus Christ; whenever they thought of Jesus Christ, they thought of God. They could not think of God without thinking of Jesus Christ; they could not think of Jesus Christ without thinking of God.

Jesus has died for us. This is the mystery of faith. But an equally great mystery is that Jesus has lived for us, and has shown us what it means to live as a Son of God.

We know that this is the way in which we ought to live, but we cannot readily discover how it is to be done. The trouble lies in the rebel will, which is part of the make up of every single one of us. This is the will of which William Temple so pungently remarked, 'I know that I can be good if I want to, but I don't want to.' How is the problem to be solved? Ever since Adam began to say 'I and me and mine', this has been with us.[3] We are familiar with all the compounds which begin with self – self-love, self-indulgence, self-gratification, self-sufficiency, self-assertion, self-realisation; there is no end to them. How is this

3. This is a theme that is extensively dealt with in a medieval work, the *Theologia Germanica*, which Martin Luther among others found very enlightening.

problem to be dealt with unless we follow Buddhism and solve the problem of the self by the total elimination of the self?

Self-realisation as an ideal has a long and respectable lineage in philosophies and religions. A good deal depends on definition – both of the meaning of the word 'self' and of the meaning of 'realisation'. If the individual self is all-important, and the salvation of the individual self is the highest of all aims, then the realisation of all the potentialities of that individual self may seem to be the aim beyond which there can be no other. 'The attainment of self-perfection will involve the full use of all the individual's "talents" or endowments, whether they be few or many, great or small, in that these may be instrumental to the greatest moralisation and perfecting of the self.'[4] This idea of individual self-perfection is found very strongly stressed in a number of eastern religions. Human relationships are to be cherished up to a certain point. But when all duties have been fulfilled, the Hindu ascetic casts aside the last object which binds him to society, that sacred thread which is the sign of his birth and his adoption as a member of one of the 'twice-born' communities, and goes out alone, independent of all others, perfectly self-sufficient, to find alone the way of perfection, of individual salvation.

Radically different from this are the forms of philosophy and religion in which 'the other' is all important. If relatedness to 'the other' is so important, self can be realised only in society, and perfect self-realisation is possible only in a perfect society. The Christian identifies the perfect society with the kingdom of God. Paradoxically, therefore, self-realisation is identifiable with perfect self-abandonment to the service of that kingdom, with perfect surrender to the will of God, whose purpose it is to bring in that kingdom.[5]

If this is true, then the paradox of the Gospel is seen to be more logical than most other ideas of the way in which we

---

4. F.R. Tennant in Hastings *ERE*, XI, p.365.
5. A secularised version of this is Kant's famous principle laid down in his *Metaphysic of Morals* (§ 11): 'So act as to treat humanity, whether in thine own person or that of any other, in every case as an end withal, never as a means only.'

ought to live. It is in losing ourselves that we really gain ourselves.

If a beginning in this direction has been made, recognition must follow that this is a beginning and no more. The Son needed time to make sure that his compass always pointed to the north; how much more will the sons need to pay time and attention to the same demand. They are exposed, as he was, to the countless distractions, often plausible, which tend to draw attention away from the centrally important things, as well as to the downward pull of a past that persistently demands recognition in the present. Sonship demands daily attention; time is not wasted if it is spent in quiet contemplation of the Son, and what sonship meant to him. The effect of such meditation is likely to be a sad awareness of the width of the angle through which our sonship has diverged from what we see sonship to have been in him, and as we know that it ought to be in us.

One question yet remains to be asked – is it possible to give precision to the idea of sonship as a practical programme for living in the world? We know in general terms what a kingdom of God would be like. It would be a realm in which no one would be hungry or cold or lonely or desolate, in which all would work for the good of each, and each for the good of all. When we attempt to come down to details, difficulties arise. Perhaps a single word of Jesus may give us the clue of which we are in search: 'Happy are the peacemakers, for they shall be called the sons of God' (Matt. 5:9). In one of the instructions to the disciples, Jesus says that, in entering a house, they are to say, 'Peace be to this house', and then the remarkable expression, 'If a son of peace be there...' What is a son of peace? Peace in the Scriptures is not simply that which comes about through the cessation of strife, but that which comes about when the will of God is perfectly done. The Son of God is the one whose own will be perfectly and inflexibly set on seeing that the will of God is carried out; it was this inflexible resolution which carried him through all the uncertainties and perplexities of life towards a goal which at the end he saw clearly to be that in the direction of which he had been moving all the time. Our wills will never be set so unalterably as was his. But, once the initial resolution has been taken – 'I come to do thy will' – may it not be reasonable to hope that enough light will fall upon our path, as on his, and that we, too, may be able to find our way to that which finally we shall see to be an appointed end?

The followers of Jesus, after his resurrection, became aware that, as he had promised, in seeing him they had seen the Father. He was the Son in whom they had been able to see the Father (Matt. 11:27). Before long they began to ask themselves how it was that in the Son they could see the Father. When did the Father begin to manifest himself in the Son? When did the Son begin to be the one in whom the Father could make himself completely manifest?

The elucidation of this problem had to wait for the period of the great fathers of the Church; but already in the New Testament there are hints that an answer had been found. God never changes. If today he is a God who shows himself, from the beginning he must have been a God who showed himself, a God whose will it was to make himself manifest to the children of men. The nature of the showing may vary, but from the beginning till the end of time its essence will be the same. On the first page of the Bible it is recorded that God spoke; speech is the means by which one personal being reveals himself to another. What did God say? 'Let there be light.' A wise expositor of this ancient Scripture interprets this as meaning 'let me be seen'.

For many generations Christians have been accustomed to listen on Christmas day to the reading of the prologue to the Gospel of St John, and many have been puzzled by the opening phrase: 'In the beginning was the Word'. Who is this Word, and what has he to do with Jesus Christ? If for the mysterious '*logos*', we read 'revelation', things become much clearer; this great passage deals with a God who desires to make himself known, and in particular wants to make himself known to the human race.

So he makes himself known in the order and beauty of the world: 'all things were made through him'. He makes himself known through the questionings of the human consciousness: 'the life was the light of men'. Human beings are that species which has the faculty of asking questions about ultimate reality, of feeling after God, if by any chance they might find him (Acts 17:27). Man is not left alone in his gropings: 'there was a man sent from God whose name was John', and he was only the last in a long line of messengers who in many fragments and in a variety of ways (Heb. 1:1) made known to the human race the wisdom and the purpose of God. And then this revealing God once for all took three-dimensional form, in which human beings might recognise their own true nature, and so recognise the nature of God: 'the Word became one of us and lived a human life like ours' (John 1:14 Gk). This life was lived only once and then was no longer seen; but the revelation has been continued through the ages in a fellowship, as in generation after generation men and women have relived the experience of seeing themselves as they are, and seeing God as he is in the face of Jesus Christ: 'the law came by Moses; but grace and truth came by Jesus Christ' (John 1:17). In him we see the reality, of which all other manifestations of God are only shadows; and in him we receive grace, that is the needed help, to live as sons of God.

'If the Son makes you free, you will be free indeed' (John 8:36). 'No one who denies the Son has the Father. He who confesses the Son has the Father also' (1 John 2:23). 'This is the true, the genuine, God and eternal life. Little children, keep yourselves from counterfeits' (1 John 5:20-21 Gk).

What was the Prophet Muhammad really repudiating?

> *What repeatedly the Qur'an disavows . . . is not the Christian doctrine of the incarnation, but the Christian heresy of adoptionism. The recurrent term is ittakhadha, with the sense 'to take to oneself' and walad (a son) as object . . . There is no doubt that the Qur'ān intends to repudiate the*

whole Christian theme of God incarnate and the words 'God resist them: how they are perverse' (9:30) are directed in imprecation against Christians, among others, because they hold that 'Messiah is the son of God'. Yet adoptionism is broadly what it has in mind. It is possible in this way to relieve the orthodox Christian faith of much of the burden of explicit Qur'anic repudiation.

Kenneth Cragg, 'Islam and Incarnation' in *Truth and Dialogue* (ed. John Hick), pp. 138–9.

7

The Friend through whom bad friends can become good friends

Aristotle tells us that good friends alone are to be chosen. If this is true, why do the Gospels call Jesus the friend of sinners?

Everyone knows what friendship is. It is so familiar that that vast repository of knowledge on almost every conceivable subject, the *Encyclopaedia Britannica*, does not include an article on it, though it has an extensive article on that Christian body which has chosen for itself the name 'the Society of Friends'. The experience, on one or other level and in one or more of the various forms that it takes, is so widely diffused that almost anyone who has a gift for writing could write well and intelligently about it; indeed so many have done so that 'there is no subject of morality which has been better handled and more exhausted than this'.[1] Generations of schoolboys have been driven through the pages of Cicero's *De Amicitia.*

Yet, when we look at it closely, friendship is seen to be not quite so simple and transparent as it may at first appear.

What is the difference between mere acquaintanceship and friendship? Clearly the words refer to the same kind of experience, but not to the same experience. The two overlap, but what is it that is distinctive in each of them?

Can friendship exist without some intrusion of what can only be called love? It is here that we are to look for the

1. The quotation is from Joseph Addison, *The Spectator,* no. 68.

difference between mere acquaintanceship and real friendship. On the whole we choose our friends. But almost everyone has had the experience of a friendship 'unasked, unhoped'[2] when what had seemed a very ordinary relationship suddenly blossoms into deep friendship, unaccountably and sometimes without apparently any of the natural emotional affinities on which so many friendships are based. Can any explanation be given of this interesting phenomenon?

Some friendships are evanescent; others show themselves to be deep-rooted and permanent. Is it possible to identify that wherein the element of permanence lies?

Those who have given close attention to this matter have found it convenient to distinguish between sentimental friendships, intellectual friendships, and religious friendships.

Sentimental friendships are unlikely to prove permanent. They are in many cases entered into without forethought, without consideration of factors other than immediate feelings and without regard for possible consequences. Feelings come and go. If the original feeling of mutual attraction fades, the friendship is really at an end, though it may be artificially maintained for a time from a sense on each side of obligation.

In intellectual friendships the mind is deeply engaged, and the basis usually includes a community of central interests and concerns. Minds continue to grow, and therefore there is a continual freshness of exchange in such friendships. History can tell us of many such. Many Johnsons have had their Boswell. In the field of biblical studies, the friendship of the three nineteenth-century biblical scholars, Lightfoot, Westcott and Hort, is famous. They managed to disagree without dissension, and worked together for many years, to the great benefit of the studies in which each was engaged and to the great advantage of the Church, until death dissolved the partnership.

---

2. The phrase comes from Cardinal Newman, but I have not been able to trace the quotation.

If we refer to religious friendships, the mind of the Christian will naturally turn to friendships in which the living Jesus is a feature. But we must not narrow the field too much. As we have seen, the Buddha had a devoted friend, Ānanda, who was with him at the time of his death. The prophet Muhammad had a slave to whom he was deeply attached, and to whom he gave his freedom. But perhaps Christians are right in thinking that Jesus revealed new dimensions of friendship, and that he is himself the element of permanence in friendship between those who believe in him.

It is a matter not of theory but of experience and observation that friendships in which Christ plays a part have a quality of durability which is less frequently found in friendships of other kinds. Friends who have found in Christ the third member in their partnership may be separated in space by many thousands of miles and long intervals of time; and yet, when they meet after a period of perhaps twenty years, they find that they can pick up the threads of friendship exactly where they laid them down, and perhaps with a degree of intimacy such as they had not previously known. They will certainly have changed in a great many ways, but he has not changed. It is that element of changelessness which has held them together and kept friendship intact against all that can be effected by the severing power of seas and years.

So in this chapter what we shall mainly be talking about is what Christ has taught, and in himself revealed, about this strange power of human friendship. But, before we come to him, it will not be a waste of time to look at what others have thought and experienced in times and situations other than those in which he lived and spoke.

The Greeks, those avid observers of human life, had a great deal to say about friendship.

In the most romantic of the surviving Greek tragedies, the *Iphigenia in Tauris*, Euripides depicts for us in moving terms the dilemma of two friends, each of whom desires to sacrifice himself to save the life of the other. Orestes and his friend Pylades have been shipwrecked on the inhospitable shores of the Crimea, and find that by ordinance of the goddess all Hellenes who arrive in that country are to be offered in human sacrifice, the priestess in charge of the rite being no other than Iphigenia, the sister of Orestes, miraculously rescued from the sacrificial knife wielded by her father Agamemnon. The young men argue persuasively, each desirous of giving his life for the sake of the other, until the dilemma is resolved by one of those tricks to which the gods and goddesses of the Greek world were not averse.

Aristotle, who wrote about everything, naturally wrote about friendship, and devoted no less than two whole books of his *Nicomachean Ethics* to the subject. As is well known, there are three Greek words for love – *agape*, which hardly enters into the argument in classical Greek, since the noun is rare, and the verb at times means little more than 'to be content with a situation', or even 'to put up with'; *erōs*, which usually, though not always, has a sexual connotation; and *philia*, which corresponds most usually to the English word 'friendship', though Aristotle does use this word in contexts where in English it would be more natural to use the term 'love'.

Aristotle has little to say about that particular kind of friendship between males, which shocked and perplexed the Victorian admirers of the Greeks, and still tends to distract the attention of English readers. Those who are charmed by Plato's vivid descriptions of the young athletes returning from the race or the wrestling bout, and of those older admirers who watch them as they return, sometimes fail to notice that almost all these admirers, like Socrates, were married men and fathers, and that they took it for granted that all these young men would, in quite a short time, grow up to be themselves married men and fathers. The aim of the older admirer is that his young friend should grow up into the finest man that he can possibly be, as soldier, as citizen, as statesman. Plato, in the *Phaedrus*, draws a highly displeasing picture of the young man who has mistaken a temporary relationship for a permanent one, and finds that he has become the object of disgust and not of pleasure to his former admirer.

With all these things Aristotle has little to do. His work is full of pertinent sayings, rather prosaic, down to earth, taking little account of the sentimental aspect of things, almost commercial in its view of the exchange between friends of profit and loss:

> It appears therefore that the company of friends is desirable in all circumstances. As the lovers find their greatest delight in seeing those they love, and prefer the gratification of the sense of sight to that of all the other senses . . . so likewise for friends . . . the society of each other is the most desirable thing that there is. For friendship is essentially a partnership. And if a man stands in the same relation as to himself, but the consciousness of his own existence is good, so also therefore is the consciousness of his friend's existence; but the consciousness is activated in companionship; hence friends naturally desire each other's society. And whatever pursuit it is that constitutes existence for a man or that makes life worth living, he desires to share that pursuit with his friends . . . the friendship of the good is good, and grows with their intercourse.[3]

It is difficult to write sensibly in the modern world about friendship, because of the sexual obsession which has beset certain sections of the English-speaking world. The shadow of this obsession tends to fall on all human relationships, so that a sexual factor is held to be dominant in every relationship between male and female, between male and male, and between female and female. Friendship in which, if the sexual element is present at all, it is minimal, whereas the delight in companionship, in mutual enrichment, is unlimited and unconfined, seems to lie outside the experience of many people today. A wider acquaintance with human nature, both in literature and in life, makes it plain that friendships of this kind

---

3. Aristotle, *Nic. Ethics,* IX, § xii, 2-3. This is from the concluding section of the study of friendship.

are in no way to be regarded as of rare occurrence; indeed any full human life is likely to be starred and bejewelled by friendships of this affectionate and lasting kind.

Many older men can rejoice in friendships which, beginning in the days of school or college, have continued through a period of half a century. In a foreword to a book by the Old Testament scholar, A. Lukyn Williams, *The Hebrew Christian Messiah* (1916), Bishop F.H. Chase of Ely refers in pleasant phrase, to a friendship which 'is hasting to fulfil its fortieth year'. Sometimes, when friends get married, the relationship changes its character and intimacy diminishes. But this is far from being always the case. Christian marriage is, in a great many cases, an enlargement of friendship, and parents and friends watch together with delight the growth of children into Christian maturity. This is not imagination. As I was planning this chapter, I found one morning on my desk a letter which came as an expression of a third generation in a family friendship which has lasted for more than sixty years.

Friendships between men and women without marriage are probably less frequent, but they do occur. In the nineteenth century, the most famous example was probably the long-continued friendship between Benjamin Jowett, the Master of Balliol College, Oxford, and Florence Nightingale. It is almost certain that Jowett proposed marriage to her; but, when she wisely refused, the friendship continued unabated. One of the odder developments in the life of Bernard Shaw was a staunch friendship between him and the Mother Superior of an order of enclosed nuns, who by diligent study had made herself a considerable authority in the field of liturgical study. Such friendships are, of course, possible only on the basis of deep mutual respect, of acceptance without any hints of aggression.

It is customary to draw a rather sharp distinction between the Hellenic and the Semitic genius, and between the cultures that grew out of these differing views of life. But Hellene and Hebrew were alike in their zest for living, and for giving memorable expression to the experiences of life. Friendship was important to the Greeks. Among the Semites friendship was a serious business, often entered into by means of a solemn covenant, ratified by the exchange of gifts. The most sinister event in Absalom's rebellion against his father David (2 Sam. 15-18) was the transfer of allegiance by Ahithophel, the king's counsellor, from his friend to the enemy of his friend. When Ahithophel's wise counsel had been rejected and he saw at once that the rebellion had failed, he realised that for him there could be no forgiveness; he went quietly home, and hanged himself (2 Sam. 17:23). When David's true friend came with feigned allegiance to the rebel, Absalom said to him with a mixture of astonishment and outrage, 'Is this your loyalty to your friend? Why did you not go with him?' (2 Sam. 16:17). Both are surpassed by Ittai the Gittite, who, though an alien, knows what the true value of friendship is. David gives him liberty to depart, 'and may the Lord ever be your steadfast friend'; but the alien will not accept this dismissal: 'As the Lord lives, and as my lord the king lives, wherever my lord the king shall be, whether for death or for life, there will your servant be' (2 Sam. 15:20-21).

Classic in the biblical story is the friendship between David and Jonathan. There is no suggestion in the narrative, though some have tried to find it there, of any homosexual element in the relationship. Certainly the terms in which the friendship between the two are expressed are not such as would fit in well with our more frigid northern temperament: 'Jonathan had given his heart to David and had grown to love him as himself. So Jonathan and David made a solemn compact because each loved the other as dearly as himself' (1 Sam. 18:2-3). But David and Jonathan were both married men, and the fathers of sons. Their friendship lasted throughout their lifetime, and was continued beyond death in David's concern for Jonathan's family. The language of David's lament for his friend – 'your love to me was wonderful, surpassing the love of women' (2 Sam. 1:26), might be thought injudicious in our suspicious century; but most of us learnt in school the meaning of the word 'hyperbole'.

Jesus had grown up in a Semitic environment, and had been

familiar from his boyhood with the Old Testament. It is hardly surprising that much of the record of his life deals with Jesus among his friends.

Remarkable in this story is the place that Jesus found for women among his companions. There is no evidence in the Bible for the kind of *purdah*, segregation of women, that is practised in many Muslim countries; but, on the whole, women in Jewish society tended to be kept in the background, as they were in the Athens of Pericles.[4] There are a surprising number of references to deep and tender affection between husband and wife – more, I think, than in the Greek tradition. Has any more touching epitaph ever been written than this: 'The word of the Lord came to me, "Son of man, behold, I am about to take the delight of your eyes from you at a stroke."... So I spoke to the people in the morning, and at evening my wife died' (Ezek. 24:15,18). Sometimes a woman could play a part of undesirable influence, as in the story of the accession of Solomon to the throne (1 Kings 1:5-31). But generally it was taken for granted that a woman's place was in the home, and that serious business was the affair of men. So the frank and open participation of women in the ministry of Jesus is something to be noted with a measure of surprise.

'There were certain women, who had been healed of evil spirits and sicknesses – Mary Magdalene, from whom seven demons had come forth' (there is no suggestion of reference to an indecorous manner of living), 'Joanna the wife of Chuza, Herod's steward, and many others who ministered to him of their substance' (Luke 8:1-3). This is the one indication in the Gospels of the financial support which made possible the itinerant ministry of Jesus. It was natural that these women of good social position were concerned with the burial of Jesus, and were the first to receive the news of his resurrection.

---

4. See the reference, in his famous speech in the *History* of Thucydides II.45: 'Great is your glory . . . and great also is hers of whom there is least talk among men whether in praise or in blame.'

There is a similar spontaneity and naturalness about the recorded friendship of Jesus with a family: 'Jesus loved Martha and her sister and Lazarus' (John 11:5). Here the strong word *agape* is used of this friendship; it speaks rather of total commitment to the well-being of others than of any emotional excitement. And, when the sisters send to tell Jesus of their brother's sickness, the less intense word is used: 'Lord, your friend is sick' (11.3 Gk). Many attempts have been made to fix with precision the meaning of the two words in every context in which they appear in the New Testament, but without success. It is one of the mannerisms of the writer of the fourth Gospel that, limited as his vocabulary is, he likes to ring the changes on words (as for example the two words for 'ask') without identifiable difference in meaning. The members of the family were just friends; it was the special quality which Jesus put into everything he did that determined the meaning, rather than a particular choice of words.

Naturally, it is in the specially chosen circle of disciples that we find in its fullest range the manifestations of the friendship of Jesus. For the most part these disciples belonged to the same social class as Jesus – not affluent, but not drawn from the ranks of the very poor. With one exception, they seem to have been all Galileans, and several we know to have belonged to the hardy race of fishermen, skilled to handle boats amid the shifting winds and the potentially tempestuous blasts which could descend suddenly from the hills on the waters of the Lake of Galilee. There was a certain equality among them. Yet, from the start, there was no doubt as to who was the leader. He had called, and they had followed. The mind of a reader may go back to the Buddha and the friends who went with him on his preaching journeys; he, too, was the one to whom they looked up with reverence, from whose lips they drank in the deeper knowledge which they still lacked. India through the centuries has celebrated the relation of affectionate intimacy which could exist between the *guru* and the *chela*, the teacher and the disciple; one of the tasks of the *chela* is to care for the physical needs of the teacher, especially if the teacher is growing old and less able to care for himself.

Aristotle discourses at some length on the problem of friendship between those who are unequal in status or abilities.[5] This argument, however, is a little artificial. There are many different kinds of inequality. A friend who is poor cannot render the same kind of services as a friend who is rich, but, if he is the superior in grace and in wisdom, he may have gifts to share of far greater value than the mere distribution of largesse. Jesus is unquestionably the leader among his friends, but it is quite clear that the friendship is not simply one-sided; it is of value to him: 'No longer do I call you servants, for the servant does not know what his master is doing; but I have called you friends' (John 15:15). In the Lucan story of the passion, twice over attention is drawn to the comfort and help that Jesus received from the presence of his friends: 'You are the ones who have stayed with me to the very end in my time of trial' (Luke 22:28 Gk). A little earlier he has said, 'With intense desire I have desired to eat this passover with you before I suffer' (Luke 22:15; the Semitic idiom 'desiring I have desired' breaks through into the Greek). It is impossible to be certain whether the last supper of Jesus with his disciples was the passover meal or not. But either of the possible interpretations of his words is appropriate: 'I desired intensely to eat this last passover with you before I die, and I have been given the joy of being with my friends for the last time; for this I am grateful.' Or it may be: 'I longed to keep the passover with you, but this has not been granted me; we must look forward to another meeting, another festival, which we shall celebrate on another shore, when all these things have been accomplished and the kingdom of God has finally come in power.'

Jesus chose his companions because of what he saw that he could make of them. But his task in educating them was not always easy. Reading the accounts, one is reminded of the remark of Ignatius Loyola about his great disciple, Francis

5. See esp. *Nic. Ethics,* VIII, § 14.

Xavier, that 'he was the stiffest dough that I have ever moulded'. Devout Jews, like their teacher, they knew the Old Testament well, and shared in the expectation of the coming of the Messiah and the great messianic days. But, friends as they were, they still found it difficult to enter into the mind of the one whom they followed, and to make themselves one with him in intention and in loyalty.

We must not be unduly hard on the poor disciples. The story is so familiar to us; we forget how much must have been strange and disturbing to them, and how much they had to learn from Jesus as they went along. We fall too easily into the error of underestimating the originality of Jesus. Even when he used ordinary and familiar words, he poured into them a wealth of new meaning. Even when he moved among men and women as one of themselves, he penetrated far more deeply into things than they did, and saw visions which, do what he could, he found it very difficult to share with them. The disciples were men of their own time, and their minds were filled with the same kind of expectations and confusions as occupied the minds of other men.

It is part of the superb veracity of Mark's Gospel that he makes no attempt to conceal the perplexities that plagued the minds of the disciples. Mark's emphasis on this aspect of the ministry has led some to suppose that his aim was polemical – to show that the true understanding of the Gospel is to be found in the Pauline interpretation, and not in the version associated with Peter and the original disciples. But such an explanation seems to be artificial. More than the other evangelists, Mark takes us back into the atmosphere of things as they were before the resurrection of Jesus. I can imagine someone saying to Peter, as he recalled the days that they had been with Jesus, 'But, Peter, could you really have been as stupid as all that?', and Peter replying, 'Yes, we were just as stupid as that.' What Mark records for us need not be understood as implying that the disciples were less than ordinarily intelligent; it is a measure of the incomparable grandeur and originality of the message which Jesus was trying to impart to them.

The deepest confusion arose from the expectation that what Jesus was about to bring in was an earthly kingdom, the throne of David once again to be established in Jerusalem, the holy city. If he sits as king, what will be the place assigned to his closest friends and companions? Repeatedly there is reference in the records to the clamorous and undignified discussion among the disciples as to who among them should be accounted the greatest. As they begin the last journey to Jerusalem, the contention breaks out among them; when Jesus asks them what they had been discussing as they journeyed, one would think that there must have been some shamed looks among them as they had to admit that they had been debating again the question who among them should be the greatest (Mark 9:33-37). The sons of Zebedee seek to get ahead of the others by approaching him with their unseemly request that they should be given a special place of honour in the coming kingdom (Mark 10:35-40). It is not surprising that the others felt indignation against the two for their effrontery (Mark 10:41); Jesus has once again to draw their attention to the secret of true greatness in the kingdom – even the Son of Man came not to be ministered to but to minister.

In the Johannine account, Jesus gives the supreme and dramatic manifestation of what it means that the one who is master and lord takes visibly upon him the form of a servant. The story opens with the moving phrase that Jesus, having loved his own who were in the world, loved them to the very end (or perfectly; John 13:1). His love and patience must often have been sorely tried – by their failure to understand, by the restless ambition which would not be stilled. But they have not worn out his love; he is ready to make one last effort to bring home to them that the way to greatness in the kingdom is to take the lowest place, to accept the position of being the servant of all. It would be hard to find in the records of any other great religious teacher outside the Christian tradition a parallel to this repeated emphasis in the teaching and in the example of Jesus.

To anyone who has lived in the East the situation will immediately become clear. Where men and women for the most part go about barefoot or in sandals, the provision of water with which to wash the feet before entering the house is taken for granted; the failure to supply it is a breach of elementary courtesy to which, in another context, Jesus draws pointed attention (Luke 7:44). A servant was usually on hand to attend to the needs of the guests. If Jesus and his disciples have sat down to supper without having washed their feet, it is clear what has happened; no servant was present, none of the disciples has taken upon him to play the part of a servant, and to minister to the needs of the others. So the Master takes upon him the form of a servant, to make up for the omission of the cleansing which would have been more in order at the beginning of the feast.

The lesson of the occasion is drawn in memorable words. Reference is often made to the Lord's two commandments – that we should love the Lord our God, and our neighbour as ourselves. This is a summary of what is laid down in the Old Testament; when the fuller meaning poured into the ancient commandments by Jesus is recognised, these will serve adequately as a guide to the whole duty of men in general. But the specific command of Jesus looks beyond these two. The new commandment he now gives is that we should love one another as he has loved us; by this will all men know that we are his disciples (John 13:34-35). He has shown through the years of his ministry just what his love for his friends is like – patient, forbearing, undemanding, tender, compassionate, always utterly reliable, stronger than death itself. This and no less is the ideal that he sets before those who wish to follow him. This is the friendship that he still makes available to those who are willing to follow, and of which they have experience in the day-to-day task of following him.

Of all the many titles given to Jesus in the Scriptures, the one that comes nearest to the hearts of men is that which was given him not by his followers but by his enemies – the friend of sinners (Matt. 11:19; Luke 7:34). Of all the features in the ministry of Jesus, this was the one that the self-righteous found most disturbing. Aristotle would have been on their side;

almost the last thing he has to say about friendship is that friendship with the undesirable is likely to be harmful to the good; he refers to what were to Greeks the well-known lines of the poet Theognis: 'From excellent persons you shall learn excellent things; if you associate with the evil, you will lose even the intelligence that you have. Realising this, be careful to associate with the good.' There is, indeed, something highly paradoxical in the approach of Jesus to sinners; they do not seem to have found his presence disturbing or humiliating; yet they are aware that the friendly welcome he accords to them does not involve any condonation of their wrongdoing, or any evasion of their need for that radical change of heart which he describes as learning to think the way God thinks.

All this is vividly summed up in the brief narrative of the Lord's visit to the house of Zacchaeus the tax-collector. The Lord knows who and what he is, and he knows that the Lord knows who and what he is. But, as far as the conversation is recorded, no word is spoken of the sins of which Zacchaeus and his kind were well known to be guilty. It just happened that Jesus was there, and something happened to Zacchaeus; the hard heart melted, an old self slipped away, and he became a new man. How did it come about? We are not told, but Jesus summed it up briefly: 'Today health and healing have come to this house, seeing that he also is a son of Abraham' (Luke 19:9 Gk). What happened to Zacchaeus has happened through the ages to countless other people.

Bishop John Robinson wrote recently (1973) a book with the attractive title *The Human Face of God.* We have said earlier that, when Christians use the term 'God', they mean by it 'the Father of our Lord Jesus Christ'. No man has seen God at any time; who and what God is remains a mystery. But here we have one whom we can know and understand, because in the reality of what theologians call the incarnation, we have one who really became one of us and shared our life (John 1:14). If he has been good enough to call us his friends, we cannot do other than take that friendship seriously.

The first thing we learn, as we set to work to get to know this friend, is that we need conceal nothing from him. We spend much of our lives playing up to one another; there is much in us that we would be glad that our friends should not know. But this friend knows it all already, and therefore it is possible for us to be completely honest with ourselves and with him. And the strange thing is that, whatever kind of a self it is that we have to show to him, this is never an occasion for despair. The verse in St John's Gospel, 'him who comes to me I will not cast out' (John 6:37) proves itself again and again to be true.

In the great medieval hymn *Dies Irae* there is much that is frankly non-Christian. But one line stands out as containing the very heart of the Gospel: '*mihi quoque spem dedisti*' – to me, even to me, thou hast given hope. It has been said, rightly, that the Christian faith is the only faith that makes a virtue of hope. Such hope is not any kind of a shallow optimism. It is based on awareness of the infinite goodness of God as shown to us in Jesus, and on a willingness to believe that the promises with which the Gospels are strewn are good coin and can be trusted. A wise Victorian poet has written, 'God shall forgive thee all but thy despair'.[6]

Professor Paul Tillich proclaimed the great principle 'believe that you are accepted, and you are accepted'. This has too often been interpreted in a sense that Tillich never intended, as though it meant that you are accepted because you are in some way acceptable. This is exactly the opposite of the truth. God's love in Christ is shown precisely in his infinite capacity for accepting the unacceptable, for recognising in Zacchaeus a son of Abraham. In Francis Thompson's once-famous poem 'The Hound of Heaven', when the chase has come to an end, the one who has fled him down the nights and down the days has to learn to recognise 'how little worthy of any love thou art', and God asks, 'Whom wilt thou find to love ignoble thee, Save Me, save only Me?' If this is true, what answer can there be other than gratitude? Gratitude is not, as some would have us

---

6. F.W.H. Myers, *St Paul.*

believe, a servile grovelling attitude; it is based simply on the recognition of certain facts – here is one who has seen in me what I never could have ventured to believe that I have in me, who has the skill to put worth upon the worthless, and to value me not because of what I am, but of what he sees that he can make of me. To have such a friend cannot be other than a source of endless surprise.

But no love that is truly love is ever tolerant of anything less than perfection in the one who is loved. Jesus creates his own dimensions of understanding what human nature is intended to be, and can become, when it is recreated after the manner of the one who has shown what it is like in its perfection. So increasing acquaintance with Christ goes hand in hand with a daunting awareness of the vast distance which still separates us from him. The real saints have a maddening habit of telling you, with St Paul, that they are really the chief of sinners. This is not pretence, or a kind of Uriah Heep arrogance in a false affectation of humility. It is simply the recognition of a fact. Living with Christ, I discover how much in me had to be forgiven, and how much is still in need of forgiveness. Our vocation is not just to avoid doing what we know to be wrong, but to live each day up to the maximum of which that day is susceptible in useful and joyful service to God and his kingdom. And who will ever say that he has lived one single day up to that level?

Our friend does not leave us in ignorance of the way in which we are to walk in order to be pleasing to the Father. There is, first, the example plainly set before us in the New Testament, and this is the objective criterion by which all our doings and attemptings are to be judged. A danger lurks in the well-known phrase 'The Imitation of Christ', the title of one of the most famous books of devotion ever written.[7] We cannot put

7. The *De Imitatione Christi* is attributed to Thomas à Kempis, a monk who lived from about AD 1380 to 1471. It seems to have been translated into English first by the Lady Margaret, mother of King Henry VII, and has since appeared in countless editions.

ourselves in the position of a Jew of the first century; we have to face a multiplicity of problems that were unknown in the pre-industrial age. Nor is it always sufficient to ask the simple question: 'What would Jesus do?' Guidance rarely comes as a sudden flash of inspiration. It comes much more through quietly pondering the nature and the will of Christ; then sometimes the mists clear, and of the two alternatives one stands out unmistakably as the one which has to be chosen. And with the clear indication comes, at times, the strength to get busy and to carry out the duty the way to which has been pointed out.

What is apparent in the way that Jesus follows to the cross is the strength and flexibility of his will. Our wills are often weak. All too often our trouble is that we see clearly enough what ought to be done, but are too supine to make the necessary effort, or too self-indulgent to exchange ease for strenuous obedience. Two are better than one; even in human affairs the presence of a friend may help us over the hump of resistance on to the upward slope of consent to what we see to be good. The presence of the unfailing friend, whose dreams and deeds were one, is just the thing needed

> the embers of our failing might
> Into a flame to fan.[8]

This friendship is one that we can never wear out. The best of human affections may fail and become feeble; the divine love burns with a clear and steady light. We may, if we will, turn our backs on the love so generously offered; there is no compulsion to comply with its demands. But if we turn again to him, we shall find that friendship always accessible, always ready to receive and to forgive. This is the point of those resurrection narratives in which it is made clear that the disciples are restored to Christ and so restored to themselves. The first word

---

8. The quotation is from a hymn by T.T. Lynch, 'I have a captain'.

spoken by the risen Christ to the disciples is, 'Peace be unto you.' Peter, who has three times denied, is three times assured that the transgression is not one that can never be forgiven. We have denied him very much more often than three times; but to us also comes the assurance that this is a love which many waters cannot quench, nor can the floods sweep it away.

The sober Aristotle tells us that the friendship of the superior is to be desired, but that the friendship of the less worthy is to be avoided because of the harmful effects that are likely to follow on such friendship. The Gospel teaches exactly the opposite. Jesus has infinite confidence in the power of goodness. 'Bad money drives out good' says the common sense of Gresham's law; the paradox of the Gospel is that goodness drives out badness. Shakespeare, who knew a thing or two about human nature, in the least successful of all his plays, *Pericles, Prince of Tyre*, depicts Marina teaching divinity in the brothel, to which she has been shamefully consigned; so successfully that Boult in indignation is fain to remark, 'The nobleman would have dealt with her like a nobleman, and she sent him away as cold as a snowball; saying his prayers too' (Act IV Scene 6).

The Gerasenes were astonished to find the man who hid himself away in the tombs, sitting at the feet of Jesus, clothed and in his right mind. There are plenty of men and women now living who can testify that what is so dramatically told in the Gospels, is equally, though perhaps less dramatically, true today.

My song is love unknown,
My Saviour's love to me,
Love to the loveless shown
That they might lovely be.
O who am I
That for my sake
My Lord should take
Frail flesh and die?

Here might I stay and sing,
No story so divine;
Never was love, dear King,
Never was grief like thine.
This is my Friend,
in whose sweet praise
I all my days
Could gladly spend.

Samuel Crossman (c.1624-84).

8

One for Many - does it make sense?

Certainly Jesus of Nazareth died. But does that make any difference to us? And, if so, what?

For more than four centuries Anglicans in all parts of the world (and Methodists also, where they have used the Anglican liturgy) have heard Sunday by Sunday the solemn words, 'who made there (by his one oblation of himself once offered) a full, perfect, and sufficient sacrifice, oblation, and satisfaction for the sins of the whole world'. The various revisions of the Book of Common Prayer have considerably modified this phraseology. Yet those who are not often in church may be startled to hear, in the Fourth Eucharistic Prayer in the Alternative Service Book put out by the Church of England in 1980, '[Jesus] made there a full atonement for the sins of the whole world, offering once for all his one sacrifice of himself'. The words and the ideas may be strange to many, but it has proved impossible to eliminate the concept of sacrifice completely from the worship of the Christian churches.

The word 'sacrifice' is used fairly frequently in ordinary speech. We speak of parents making sacrifices to ensure the education of their children – giving up advantages for themselves in order that others may gain advantage. If we have sold something we value at less than we judge it to be worth, we are likely to say that we have let it go at a sacrifice. But, if we hear the word used in a religious or quasi-religious sense, as when Kipling wrote in his 'Recessional',

Still stands Thine ancient sacrifice,
An humble and a contrite heart,
this may jar on our twentieth-century ears.

If we are thus shocked or startled, it may mean that we have not understood the immense part that the idea and the practice of sacrifice have played in the thoughts and worship of the human race as far back as we can trace clearly human consciousness. Christianity is at one with other systems of belief; here is a notable point of contact, and contrast, with those other systems.

Volumes of immense learning have been written on the origins of sacrifice, and much still remains obscure. But it seems likely that one at least of the sources is simply the feeling of sharing, of giving. Among many peoples, not excluding some on a very high level of civilisation, there exists the feeling that there are unseen members of the community, no less important than the visible members. These may be called gods, or spirits, or ancestors; but, whatever the name given, these unseen participants have their share in the concerns of the community and these must not be neglected. The Romans had their Lares and their Penates; the latter most probably intimate dwellers in the house, the former more associated with the wider community and the guardianship of the farms and the fields. No South Indian village is without its Ayyanar, the friendly guardian who at night rides round the village on his terracotta horse to keep all safe. Such spirits must be remembered, and at the appropriate time the due offerings must be made to them.

As we have seen, for a great many African peoples the ancestors play an immensely important part in the life of the tribe or race. They are entitled to a share in all the good things which the tribe enjoys; at the right time their share must be given to them. If this duty is neglected, the ancestors may be angry, and may vent their spite on those who have so far forgotten their duty towards them. For such participation the term 'oblation, offering' is perhaps more suitable than 'sacrifice'.

The Hindus had a wide and varied tradition of sacrifice, going back to the earliest days in their religion.

In Hindu mythology the universe and all that is in it owes its origin to a sacrifice offered by the gods. The victim was the man *(purusa).* From this sacrifice the gods obtained the clarified butter, out of which came the beasts which live in the air, in the forest and in villages; horses also were born from it and cows and goats and sheep. This was not all. From this sacrifice there came into being the three elements – verses, chants, ritual formulae – out of which the Vedas, the ancient sacred books, were constituted, and with them also the *dharmas*, the norms which make up the ideal order of the world. No indication is given of the one to whom the sacrifice is offered – the gods themselves are the offerers. The mysterious words in which the sacrifice is described express a profound sense of the mysterious power that resides in death, dismemberment, and the various parts of the sacrificial offering.

In later days, blood sacrifices ceased to be offered in the great temples of Hinduism; in early times they played almost a central role in worship. The culmination of sacrifice was the horse-sacrifice, which could be offered only by a king, and only by one who had never been vanquished in war. The steed chosen for the offering was to be allowed to wander freely for a year. The ceremonies attendant on the sacrifice are described in the ritual books in the greatest of detail. The doubt, however, remains as to whether this sacrifice was ever really offered.

The same doubt attaches even more strongly to that which follows in the books – the *purusa medha* or human sacrifice. Human sacrifice has certainly existed among many peoples, including those by whom the Hebrews in the early days of the occupation of Palestine were surrounded. In many cases this is regarded as the most powerful of all rituals, exercising almost coercive powers on the gods themselves. Indologists are divided in their opinion. Some of great authority, but not all, hold that though this may never have been practised in historic times, it stands in the sacred books as a kind of fossilised memory from a more barbaric period of Hindu existence.

We need not try to settle the question. What does become

clear in old Hindu traditions is the self-interested attitude of the one who offers the sacrifice. If he gives, it is in order that he may receive; he offers generously, but he expects a return that will be commensurate with his offering.

As theory developed out of practice, the general view of the relationship between men and gods is that the sacrificer can persuade, or even coerce, the god into granting whatever he may desire. This is the typically magical view; man can acquire in some mysterious way the knowledge of the *vāc*, the mystic word which, together with the appropriate actions, gives him power over the hidden forces of the universe. Man is the master, and these forces are the servant; religion, as distinct from magic, begins only when the worshipper regards himself as the servant, who puts himself at the disposal of the one who is worshipped for the fulfilment of his purposes.

Probably to most readers of this book the sacrificial rites of the Hebrews are more familiar than the recollections of distant places and very different times. In the laws of Israel, there are archaic elements; but, by the time that the Old Testament reached its present form, the sacrificial system had reached a somewhat definite and systematised form. No less than five elements have to be distinguished.

There was the annual commemorative sacrifice of the Passover, in which the people of Israel relived together the tremendous experiences of the deliverance from Egypt.

There was the daily sacrifice, morning and evening, of a lamb, in which the covenant between God and his people was renewed. In this connection it was laid down that 'fire on the altar shall be kept burning on it; it shall not go out.' (Lev. 6:12,13.)

Then, thirdly, there was the sin or guilt offering. If a trespass had been committed inadvertently by the people or by an individual, God had provided a means of reconciliation through sacrifice. The basic idea is that of 'covering'. Defilement has taken place, and is offensive in the sight of God; by the offering of blood the defilement is covered and God turns his eyes away from it. In the specially solemn rites of the day of atonement, defilement is dealt with in two ways – by the carrying of the blood of one animal into the most holy place, and by the driving away of the scapegoat into the wilderness to carry far away the sins of the people.[1]

In the burnt offering, the whole of the victim is offered to the Lord and consumed. The offerer disclaims any share in it. He is to lay his hand on the head of the victim, as though to identify himself with it, and then to kill it. (It is not the priest who immolates the victim; his role is subsidiary.) The offering is a sign of the total dedication of the offerer to the will and to the service of God.

Finally, the peace-offering rounds off the main types of sacrifice. In this God has his share, but the offerer and his family, and the priests, too, have their share, and join in the solemn feast in the presence of God. Joyful celebration was a part of the worship of Israel's God; thanksgiving to him as the author of all good things, and in some sense as the host at this shared feast in his presence, seems the most natural interpretation of the texts which deal with the peace-offering.

Already in the period of the Old Testament there were evidences of discontent in the minds of many serious people with the ritual of the tabernacle and later of the temple, and protests in favour of a more spiritual understanding of religion. In Psalm 50 we read, 'If I were hungry, I would not tell you; for the world and all that is in it is mine. Do I eat the flesh of bulls, or drink the blood of goats? Offer to God a sacrifice of thanksgiving, and pay your vows to the Most High' (12-14). In one of the greatest utterances of the whole prophetic canon, Micah puts, and answers, the question of how a man is to approach God: 'Will the Lord be pleased with thousands of rams, with ten thousand rivers of oil? Shall I give my first-born for my transgression, my children for my own sin? God has told you what is good; and what is it that the Lord asks of you? To

---

1. In more modern translations, 'scapegoat' has been replaced by the not easily intelligible 'for Azazel' (Lev. 16:8,10).

do justly, to love mercy, and to walk humbly with our God' (Mic. 6:7-8 Heb.).

During the period of exile in Babylon, there was extensive codification of the laws. With the restoration and the building of the second temple, sacrifice seemed to play almost the pre-eminent role in the religious life of the people of Israel. The more spiritual aspects of the inner life were not forgotten; but it was the splendid ritual of the temple which caught the eye. Just how this appeared to a devout worshipper is set out in the magnificent paean in which the son of Sirach depicts Simeon, son of Jochanan, the high priest:[2]

> When he put on his gorgeous vestments,
> robed himself in perfect splendour,
> and went up to the holy altar,
> he added lustre to the court of the sanctuary . . .
> he held out his hand for the libation cup
> and poured out the blood of the grape,
> poured its fragrance at the foot of the altar
> to the Most High, the King of all . . .
> Then Simeon came down and raised his hands
> over the whole congregation of Israel,
> to pronounce the Lord's blessing,
> proud to take his name on his lips;
> and a second time they bowed in worship
> to receive the blessing from the Most High.
>
> (Ecclus. 50:11-21 NEB)

This was the kind of worship which was carried out in the days of Jesus of Nazareth. He must have been familiar with it, and have seen it from time to time in his visits to the temple.

In AD 70, Jerusalem was captured by the Romans and the temple was destroyed. The sacrifices ceased, since there was no

---

2. In the English translations he is called Simon son of Onias, this being the Greek form of the names. He died about 198 BC.

place other than the Holy Place in Jerusalem where they could be offered. This was less of a disaster for the Jewish people than might have been thought, since in the two centuries before the time of Christ the synagogue, with its regular services of worship and teaching, and its extensive educational activity, had developed everywhere among the Jews scattered throughout the empire. Through the long centuries of exile the synagogue, more than any other single religious institution, has held the Jewish people together, and maintained the integrity of their life.

But, now that the Jews have returned to Jerusalem and have set up again their independent state, what is to happen? For the moment the question is in abeyance, since the Jews very wisely have not interfered with the Muslims in their possession of the sacred site on which of old the Jewish temple stood. The Dome of the Rock is still one of the most sacred sites of Islam; it is the Muslim creed which echoes within its walls, and not the *Shema* of the Hebrews.[3] But supposing that, at some future date, the Jews were to oust the Muslims and to recover the sacred places, what decision will be made regarding the ancient law of the Jews? Is the sacrificial system to be restored in its entirety? Will the Jews arrange to offer a lamb at morning and at evening in token of their covenant relationship with God? Or are such ancient customs to be reckoned obsolete and no longer obligatory?

On this question there are deep divisions among the Jews themselves. There are among them those who believe that the Torah is in every respect divine; there are to be no departures from its ordinances, when these can possibly be fulfilled. A majority, however, would probably be content to take a less literal view. Much in the Old Testament can be taken as symbolic; the spiritual or mystical sense can be given preeminence over the literal. The cessation of sacrifice is a fact of history; to attempt to reintroduce it in its literal and physical

---

3. 'Hear, O Israel, the Lord thy God is one God' (Deut. 6:4).

sense of the immolation of animals would be retrogressive and anachronistic. The spiritual realities of Jewish worship, as these have evolved through the centuries, must be preserved, and can be expanded and adapted to all the needs of the modern world.

We may without discourtesy ask our Jewish friends on what authority they rely for the abrogation of so much that is a part of their national history, and for the adoption of principles that would seem to bring them much nearer to the Christian ideas of worship than to their own historical tradition.

To some of our Jewish friends the situation may seem perplexing. Christians experience no such perplexity. All partial, typical and symbolic sacrifices have ceased to be offered, since they have been superseded and rendered unnecessary by the one perfect sacrifice which has been offered once for all on behalf of all men.

This idea is expanded at length in the Epistle to the Hebrews. The key word of this Epistle is *ephapax*, once for all, which, with the simpler form *hapax*, once only, occurs eleven times in the Epistle. The perpetual repitition of the Jewish sacrifices is the sign of their imperfection. They could show, but they could not effect. They served as a reminder once a year of the reality and seriousness of sin, but they could not achieve a finality of deliverance. The blood of bulls and of goats cannot take away sin (10:2-4). Christ's self-offering is radically different in kind. It can only happen once: 'once, in the crisis of the ages he was made manifest for the putting away of sin by the sacrifice of himself' (9:26 Gk). By this perfect sacrifice he has lifted those who trust in him out of the old world of frustration and unfulfilled desire, into the perfect liberation of a world in which sin has been overthrown and achievement of all good things is possible.

The minds of the early Christians were full of thoughts and memories of sacrifice. Even if they had never been to Jerusalem and seen the temple, they had been fed on the Old Testament. Those of them who had come in from the pagan world were familiar with all the rituals of pagan sacrifice. It was for them natural to draw on sacrificial terms in their attempts to understand and explain the meaning of what Christ has achieved for us by his death. For us who live in a different world, the terms and the ideas may be a hindrance rather than a help as we try to understand something that we know to be of great significance, but the meaning of which does not readily become clear to us.

One of the central ideas in sacrifice, that of the whole burnt-offering in which nothing is kept back and everything is given to God, causes us little difficulty. What Christ offered to the Father was the whole of himself, in the perfect union of his will with the will of the Father. The blood of bulls and goats could never take away sin, since they lacked the very thing which could have made sacrifice a reality and not a symbol – free will and the deliberate choice of death rather than life.

The connection between the death of Christ and the idea of the peace-offering has not been too difficult to trace. Many times Jesus had eaten with his friends. As their teacher and guide he must many times have taken the place of the father of the family. At sabbath dinner in a pious Jewish home, the moment at which the father takes the sabbath loaf, blesses God, solemnly breaks it and divides it among the members of the family, and offers thanks to God over the cup of wine before he hands it round to those who are present, has a special solemnity. This ritual seems certainly to have existed in the time of Jesus; on many occasions he may have used the very same blessing as is used in the Jewish family today: 'Blessed art thou, O Lord our God, King of the Universe, who causest to come forth bread from the earth; Blessed art thou, O Lord our God, who hast given us the fruit of the vine.'

On the last occasion on which he broke bread with his friends, Jesus, knowing that it was the last time, gave to the thanksgiving a special solemnity by associating it with his death: 'Take, eat; this is my body. . .' When all had drunk from the cup, he added, 'This is my blood of the covenant which is poured out on behalf of many.' This action and these words were never forgotten, not unnaturally in view of the solemnity of the occasion.

What was new in Christian worship was the regular

commemoration of the death of Christ with the recitation of the words that he had used. The ancient world was familiar with ritual feasts, sometimes held in the temple, or in the presence of the god or goddess. It is possible that these feasts of the mystery religions exercised some influence on the development and on the language of Christian worship. But the historic connection was never forgotten by Christians. The last supper of Jesus with his disciples took place at the passover season – whether it was an actual passover meal or an anticipation of it is a question on which scholars are not yet agreed. What is certain is that the minds of all will have been full of the memories of the great deliverance in which Israel came out of Egypt, and was constituted as a nation by the Lord who had delivered them. Jesus underlined the connection by his reference to the covenant which had been made between God and his people at that time. That covenant had been inaugurated by the blood of animal victims, 'Moses took the blood and threw it upon the people, and said, "Behold the blood of the covenant which the Lord has made with you in accordance with all these words"' (Exod. 24:8). Jesus is about to inaugurate a new covenant, a new deliverance, and this will be brought in through the blood of a victim far more august than the bulls and goats which were slain according to the Old Testament law.

This simple ceremony has become associated with many and varied depths of Christian meaning, and has come to be known by a great variety of names. Anglicans have been taught by their Book of Common Prayer to know it as 'the Lord's Supper' or 'Holy Communion'. To many Christians, familiar as they are with many other names, 'the Lord's Supper' is still the favourite designation for the gathering of Christians when they meet to do what the Lord asked them to do in remembrance of him. From the earliest days of the Church, Christians had been taught that, from the coming of the Holy Spirit on the day of Pentecost, the risen Christ through the Spirit was present with them at all times and in all places. But they were specially aware that he was with them when they met to do just what he had asked them to do. This presence is magnificently symbolised in the book of Revelation in the picture of the risen Christ in the midst of the seven lamps which represent the seven churches (Rev. 1:12).

Unfortunately, a great deal of ink has been spilt trying to determine the exact nature of the presence of the risen Christ in this family meal, concentrating all too often on the gifts of Bread and Wine rather than on the one who is the Giver. During the centuries, Christians of another tradition have been taught to direct their attention more to the Giver than to the gifts. Who is it who is present at the meal, and what is he there to do? If our eyes were opened to see the reality behind sign and symbol, we would see the risen Christ himself as the host, the faithful head of the family, the one who again and again gathers the faithful round himself. And what is the gift that he gives? It is simply the gift of himself, to be *esca viatorum,* the food of wayfaring travellers, on their way from the confusions of this world to the endless tranquillity of the eternal world, where signs and symbols have ceased to be because they have served their turn and are no longer needed. Just how he gives himself remains a mystery, and there is no need for us to know. That wise woman, the first Queen Elizabeth, summed up the mystery and the reality in four simple lines:

> Christ was the word who spake it;
> He took the bread and brake it;
> And what his word doth make it,
> That I believe and take it.

The equally wise theologian, Richard Hooker, wrote that, when we come to that feast at which he is the host, all we have to say is, 'Oh my God, thou art true, Oh my Soul, thou art happy.'

We run into much greater difficulty when we encounter the affirmation that Jesus Christ was made a sin-offering, that he died for our sins.

The last thing that modern individuals want is that anyone

should do anything for them. They want to be on their own, to stand on their own feet and do everything for themselves. If there is a price to be paid for what the Church calls sin, they will pay it themselves; insufferable that it should be supposed that anyone else can pay it for them.

The Muslim joins in with his reminder, when it is suggested to him that the death of Jesus has anything to do with the forgiveness of sins. He puts it rather coarsely, 'If one man eats, will another man's belly be filled?' Islam, it is maintained, is a religion for grown-up people. Stand on your own feet, and by obedience to God become the master of your own destiny.

Life is not really quite as simple as that. Whether we like it or not, other people are doing things to us and for us, and we are doing things to and for other people, whether they know it or not. It is strange that so little has been written on the subject of influence; in a *Dictionary of Christian Ethics*, which stands on my shelves, there is no article on the subject. And yet this is among the most certain of the circumstances by which we are surrounded, and, invisible and immeasurable as it may be, almost the most powerful. No man is an island; we are part of the human race. Whether we will it or no, influence good or evil is pouring out from us all the time in all directions; and in a very real sense what we do, for good or evil, we do for the whole universe. One thinker who saw this clearly and gave expression to it was the American pragmatist, William James (1842–1910). He wrote that when in the moral struggle, we gain the upper hand, we know that the whole universe is a better place for our victory, and, when we lose, we know that the whole universe is impoverished.

What we do, we do for the whole race of mankind. Where one has gone ahead, it is certain that others will be able to follow. It used to be taken as certain that no human being could swim across the English Channel. When Captain Webb achieved it (1875), it became clear that the impossible had become the possible. Now even teenagers take it for granted that that is something that they can also do, if they try hard enough. For a long time Mount Everest eluded all the strength and skill of the climbers. When Queen Elizabeth II woke on the morning of her coronation, the first thing that she was told was that Hillary and Tenzing had stood on the highest point of the world's surface. Now we have lost count of the number of times that Everest has been climbed; it is still possible to count the number of times that it has been climbed 'without oxygen'.

C.S. Lewis once made a very shrewd comment in relation to the question, 'Why did Jesus die?' He said that Jesus saw that we all had some dying to do, and he died to show us how it is done. To put it in New Testament language, we have to die to self if we are to live to God. That is exactly what he did: 'The death he died he died to sin, once for all, but the life he lives he lives to God' (Rom. 6:10).

We can pursue this picture a little further in relation to the idea of the forgiveness of sins.

Hinduism, traditionally, has denied the possibility of forgiveness. Everything is ruled by *karma*, the iron law of retribution. By action you incur debts; you and you alone can pay those debts; if you have not paid them off in this life, you must be born again and again into the world, until your accounts are finally balanced. 'Be sure your sin will find you out,' says the Old Testament (Num. 32:23). 'Although you send forth the tender calf amid many cows, it has unerring skill to seek out its own mother. Deeds of old days have ever the power to search him out to whom their fruit pertains' (*Nāladiyar*, 101). There can be no forgiveness; if God were to forgive, he would be undermining the unalterable ethical structure of the universe. (The Greek idea of *anangke*, unchangeable necessity, is not very different from this.)

So the difference between the Hindu concept and the Christian can be expressed in four simple words. Hinduism says:

You sin; you pay.

In the Christian Gospel God says:

You sin; I pay.

In the world of distributive justice, this makes simple nonsense. But the world of personal relations is governed by a different law. Men and women do sometimes forgive one another. What happens when A forgives B? Jesus makes the problem viable and measurable by two illustrations from the world of debt and remission of debt. When a creditor remits a debt which is due to him, he transfers the loss to himself, and literally pays for the pleasure of forgiving the other. It is less easy to see the logic of the situation when the offence is of a different kind, for example calumny or slander, where the injury caused is literally immeasurable. But the American theologian, Horace Bushnell (1802–76), was right when he wrote that the cross represents the cost of forgiveness to God. To forgive is no easy thing, especially when the wrong is of its very nature unforgivable.

One who really forgives goes even further than this. He stands in on the side of the one who has done the wrong to give him the assurance that he can stand up and start all over again. He makes himself one with the offender in his sense of guilt (not in the actual guilt, that is something that is non-transferable, it always remains with the one who has done the wrong and no one else), in the shame and humiliation that he may have brought upon himself, in wasted powers and opportunities, in whatever else the consequences of wrong-doing may be. The operative word is that 'he stands in with him' – not as a policeman to guard against future transgressions, not as an intolerably superior person contrasting his own virtue with the soiled reputation of the other, but as the friend who lives in hope, and rejoices in every sign that the healing power of his love and friendship is having the intended effect.

Such friendship is rare among human beings, but it exists. That it does exist encourages Christians to be confident that when they say, 'I believe in the forgiveness of sins', they are not talking nonsense, but are simply affirming something that is self-evident, if God is such as Jesus of Nazareth has declared him to be.

When Jesus lived on earth, people found it very hard to believe that he really loved sinners. The inveterate belief even of most Christians is that God really loves respectable people; they find it very hard to believe that he stands on the side of sinners, rags and all. Jesus himself said that 'greater love has no man than this, that a man lay down his life for his friends' (John 15:13). Paul rashly and almost outrageously carries this a stage further: 'greater love hath no man than this, that a man lay down his life for his enemies.' But, in fact, this is almost exactly what he says – 'at the right time Christ died for the ungodly... God shows his love for us in that while we were yet sinners, Christ died for us... while we were enemies we were reconciled to God' (Rom. 5:6,8,10). Strange. But, if it really is the case that, at the moment of crucifixion, he said, 'Father, forgive them, for they know not what they do', it might after all be true.

That is not the last word, 'If you forgive men their trespasses, your heavenly Father will also forgive you; but if you do not forgive men their trespasses, neither will your Father forgive your trespasses' (Matt. 6:14-15). We are not creatures that easily forgive the wrongs that others do to us. When I was a very small boy, I read a story in which it was reported to parents that Master Henry refused to say his prayers. What was wrong? This was the story. Henry had a little dog whom he loved very dearly; a tramp had stolen his dog. When he came to say his evening prayer, he found that he could not forgive the tramp who had stolen his dog, and so he could not say, 'Forgive us our trespasses'. I knew that, if I were Henry, I would not be able to forgive the tramp that had stolen my dog. So how could I be a Christian? That is still the problem.

So how can this chapter end, other than with the ancient prayer *Kyrie, eleison; Christe, eleison; Kyrie, eleison.*

No other of the great religions offers this atoning

sacrifice of an incarnate God. All the rest appear to think that the condition of sincere repentance and amendment is enough... It might be, if sin were merely a kind of error which could be retrieved by second thoughts, or a passing infection which our essentially healthy constitution could throw off. It is thus that most of the great religions regard it; they dare not do otherwise, or they would find the problem insoluble. But Christianity takes a graver view... For our deliverance we need the injection into our lives of a new power, a power not native to us but capable of remaking us, a power which Christ alone could and did supply; and he supplied it by his Passion and death.

H.A. Hodges, *Death and Life have contended* (1946), p.66.

9

Saviour from What? Saviour for What?

Modern man does not want to be saved. Is he right, or is there something that he has overlooked?

Some years ago a highly educated Hindu wrote to a Christian friend, 'India is now ready to accept Jesus Christ as one of the saviours of mankind.' One of the saviours, or the Saviour? Everything turns on the slight change of expression.

In the *Bhagavadgita,* the Song of the Lord, Krishna, serving as the charioteer of the hero Arjuna, but now revealed as the incarnation of the Supreme, makes plain to Arjuna that he has appeared time and time again on earth:

> For whenever the law of righteousness withers away and lawlessness arises, then do I generate myself [on earth]. For the protection of the good, for the destruction of evil-doers, for the setting up of the law of righteousness I come into being age after age.
>
> (*Bhagavadgita,* IV.7)

The many incarnations of the Hindu challenge comparison with the single incarnation in which Christians profess belief.

Nature religions are cyclical in character. They return again and again to the point of departure, just as the seasons recur in their endless and orderly sequence. The mystery religions of the Roman Empire, with their figure of the dying and rising god, are clearly related to the death of the world in winter and its rebirth in spring. The Stoics believed in a universal return, in which all things will come back to that which they were. Hinduism has its four ages; we live in the *Kali-yuga*, the fourth and degenerate age, which will last a very long time; but there is no consummation, all things begin again and the sequence is repeated. The Buddhist is pleased with the picture of universes endlessly succeeding one another, and is inclined to pity the poor Christian who has to be content with only one.

Judaism, Christianity and Islam are historical religions – each believes in a beginning, a history and an end. This does not rule out the possibility that God may have under his care countless other universes of which with our present limited senses we can have no awareness at all. We speculate on the possibility of life of very different forms in other planets, as in the charming fantasies of C.S. Lewis; there could be a *Perelandra*, in which the woman is tempted and rises superior to temptation. Alice Meynell in her poem 'Christ in the Universe', draws our vision further afield, to the various forms in which Christ may have trodden distant constellations of our universe:

> Doubtless we shall compare together, hear
> A million alien Gospels, in what guise
> He trod the Pleiades, the Lyre, the Bear.

Imagination even considers the possibility that there may be universes so different in kind from ours that it is vain even to attempt to speculate what they may be like.

For the moment, we have only one universe under scrutiny. Some, but perhaps rather few, believe in the eternity of the universe. Most think that the universe had a beginning. A considerable number of scientists favour the idea of the 'big bang', a tremendous explosion of energy in an unimaginably remote past, out of which, in course of time, all things that we can observe have come into being. A fascinating work, *The First Three Minutes,* written with a scientific and no particular religious interest, depicts for us what that first explosion may have been like, and outlines the processes of development that may have taken shape in those first crucial minutes.

Here we are still in the world of theory, and at best of probability. When we come a little nearer to our own time and to our own familiar planet, we are faced with the simple fact that there is something called history. Things happen, and, when they have happened, not even God can cause them not to have happened. I can cross out the word which I have just written, but not even God can cause me not to have written it. God may perhaps trammel up the consequence, and make the outcome to be different from what human wisdom might have foreseen or expected. But we are left with the sober reflection of Bishop Joseph Butler: 'Things are what they are, and their consequences will be what they will be; why then should we desire to be deceived?'

There is a terrible finality about history. It deals with the unpredictable, the unique, the unalterable, the unrepeatable, the irreversible. There are similarities between events and periods, and comparison is often illuminating. But history flows in one steady stream; and will move forward to whatever may be its appointed end. The adherents of the historical religions think, accordingly, in terms of one God, one universe, one human race, one history of that race, one central point of history, and one final point to which all things tend. For Christians, the central point of history is the death and ressurrection of Jesus Christ.

What gives these events their central position is that they are seen as the meeting point of the movement of God towards man, and of the upward movement of man towards God. God has spoken endlessly to man – in the ordered beauty of creation, in dream and vision, in poetry and prophecy, in judgment and promise, in the faithfulness with which he keeps the world in existence and human beings within their world. The human creature, from very early beginnings, has been able to ask the question about God, and to seek after answers to the ultimate questions, though at times the answers he has found have been crude and hardly worthy of the greatness of the questions. Man has turned to the unseen powers in prayer and ritual and sacrifice, in refusal to regard death as the final answer to all things, in all that he has been able to create of beauty and splendour to dignify the brief period of his dwelling on earth.

The human race seeks God; God equally seeks the human race. In Jesus Christ the turning of God towards the human race, and the turning of the human race towards God, have perfectly met. God in times past spoke to preceding generations in many fragmentary revelations and in many manners of self-revelation. But now, after the long period of waiting and preparation he has spoken to us in one who is appropriately called 'Son' (Heb. 1:2 Gk).

Of the various metaphors which may be used to make this concept clear, one which may appeal to modern man is that of the cantilever bridge. The two arms of the bridge descend in an ever-closer approach the one to the other; when the two interlock the bridge is made; the heavier the weight placed upon it, short of causing complete collapse, the more strongly will it hold together in one. It is safe for traffic from one side to the other; two worlds which have existed in separation have now been brought together inseparably into one. This is what the writers of the New Testament mean by the word 'salvation'.

It is surprising that the title 'Saviour' is used in the New Testament only rather rarely of Jesus Christ. Perhaps there was a feeling among the writers of that time that there were altogether too many saviours about in the world, and that the use of the term might obscure rather than make clear the uniqueness which they wish to attribute to Jesus. Grateful cities might give the title *Sotēr*, Saviour, to some potentate or other wealthy man who came to their relief in time of earthquake or other disaster. Many of the gods of the mystery religions, who seemed to hold out to frail human beings a hope of immortality, were known as saviour gods. But the term could have much wider connotations. Asclepius, the healing god, in whose temple sick persons used to go and sleep in order to be healed of their diseases, frequently bore the title 'saviour'. If Poseidon, the god of the sea, was kind enough to remain calm and give mariners a safe journey to the haven where they would be, they might make a votive offering to him in gratitude to Poseidon the saviour. In a notable passage of the *Agamemnon* of Aeschylus, describing the journey of the Achaean warriors home from Troy to their own countries, 'good luck that keeps men safe' kindly sat upon the prow of the ship that was in peril (*Agamemnon* 664.).

Such a multiplicity of saviours might conceal the one whom Christians wished to proclaim.

On the other hand, both the verb *sōzein*, to save, and the noun *sotēriā* are frequently used in the New Testament and in a variety of senses. The basic meaning seems to be to put things right when they have gone wrong. At times the meaning is less than technical: 'thy faith hath saved thee' means no more than that sickness is an abnormal state for a human being, and that now, through faith and the healing power of Christ, that which is normal has been restored. When the Philippian jailer, in the midst of the earthquake, says to Paul and Silas, 'Sirs, what shall I do to be saved?' (Acts 16:30), what he really means, translated into ordinary speech, is simply, 'Gentlemen, will you kindly tell me what I am to do to get out of this mess?' If this is what he meant, he got a good deal more than he bargained for. But in other contexts a far deeper meaning is indicated, as in 1 Peter 1:9-10 (Gk) 'receiving that good thing to which your faith looked forward, namely the salvation of your souls; and concerning that salvation prophets sought out and enquired.'

Salvation can be referred to in the past, or in the present, or in the future.

The writers of the New Testament make no concealment of their conviction that in Jesus Christ the decisive event of all the ages has taken place. It is this division of the epochs that is so puzzling to our Jewish friends – they simply reckon according to the putative age of the world, with no division, neither before nor after. Jesus was no doubt a great teacher, whom the Jews are learning in our day to reverence as never before; but in what sense could one prophet play so decisive a role in human history as to divide that history into two?

Our Muslim friends are much nearer to us than the Jews. They also have their before and after. Everything dates from the *Hijra*, the departure of Muhammad from Mecca for Medina in what we call the year AD 622. In their calendars everything is marked AH, though confusingly to Christians, since they use the lunar calendar of three hundred and sixty days and their years do not correspond with ours. It is interesting to note that for centuries Christians did not distinguish between 'before' and 'after'; they continued to reckon, as did the rest of the Roman world, from the supposed date of the foundation of Rome, 753 BC; only in the sixth century with the work of a somewhat obscure monk, Dionysius Exiguus (who incidentally got his dates wrong), were BC, before Christ, and AD Anno Domini, firmly inscribed in our calendars and our history books.

The apostles were not very good at chronology; they leave us in a state of infuriated ignorance as to the exact date at which a number of important things happened; we cannot fix for certain the year in which Christ was born or the year in which he died. But they were very good at theology; they have left us in no doubt whatever as to the meaning of the 'before' and the 'after' as they understood it.

If any man is in Christ, the new creation is already here; so St Paul in 2 Corinthians 5:17. This concept of the new creation is present in many passages in the Epistles. The first word which God speaks in the Bible is, 'Let there be light' (Gen. 1:3). The light which appears on the first page of the Bible reappears on the last in Revelation 22. Once again it is Paul who specifically links the light of creation with the light of Christ: 'It is God who said, "Let the light shine out of darkness," who has shone forth in our hearts with a view to the illumination of the knowledge of the glory of God in the face of Jesus Christ' (2 Cor. 4:6 Gk). We are told by one of the latest writers of the New Testament that we await new heavens and a new earth, in which righteousness will dwell (2 Peter 3:12-13). This is true; but faith will affirm that the new heavens and the new earth are already here, because Jesus has risen from the dead.

No metaphor is too bold for the apostolic writers to use when they want to give expression to the transition from the old world to the new. With the resurrection of Jesus Christ, a new power was let loose in the world. That power is still at work. The resurrection of Jesus Christ at one particular point in history is the supreme manifestation of the power of God. But that power is still at work in the believer. His deliverance from the world of sin and death is a little resurrection (Eph. 1:19-20). Just as Christ was raised from the dead by the glory of the Father, so we also are to walk in newness of life (Rom. 6:4). The most dramatic expression of this existential change is put in the mouth of Jesus himself: 'Except a man be born again, he cannot see the kingdom of God' (John 3:3). No wonder that Nicodemus is aghast at the suggestion; as a teacher of the Jewish law he has never heard such things.

The bridge has been built. Heaven and earth are at one. Without doubt salvation has been finally and decisively achieved. But does it look as though this really was the case? Does the world look as though it was redeemed?

This is, perhaps, the harshest gravamen that our Jewish friends bring against the Christian faith. How can we say that Messiah has come, when there is not the smallest sign that we are living in the messianic age? Martin Buber (1878–1965), a friend of Christians if ever there was one, says poignantly that the Jew feels in his own body that the world has not been redeemed, that no redemption has taken place. It is not surprising that a Jew who had lived through Hitler's holocaust in Germany should feel in this way. Christians must take such objections very seriously. We are called above all things to be realists – to look at things exactly as they are, and not to be content with simplistic or triumphalist explanations. On the meaning of the word 'redemption', however, we have two things to say.

To be redeemed does not mean to live in a land flowing with milk and honey, a land from which all sorrow and suffering have been miraculously removed. It means to take up the cross of the Redeemer daily and to carry it with him until the very end of the age. All too often we present to young people an emollient view of the Gospel; the new American Prayer Book has completely removed from the baptism service the words 'and to fight manfully under his banner against sin, the world and the devil, and to continue Christ's faithful soldier and servant until his life's end'. Surely if ever there was a time when those words were needed, it is today. During the Second World War, Churchill was right in seeing that the decisive victory had been won, when the Japanese attacked Pearl Harbor; but there was a terribly long downward slope until the fruits of that victory were finally seen. There was plenty of need to go on fighting valiantly.

Secondly, it seems to be always God's method to work from small to great. When life first appeared on this planet, almost certainly it appeared in tiny forms, threatened and vulnerable in the extreme; and yet it survived, and shows itself in the marvellously varied forms that we can see today. A single man is called out of his city, Ur of the Chaldees, and told that he is to become a great nation

(Gen. 12:1-6). Most improbable, and yet it happened. From Abraham to Moses, from Moses to David, from David to the second temple, the story of Israel expands, until it culminates in David's son who is to be the Messiah. The Church of Jesus Christ begins with a group of frightened Jews in an upper room in Jerusalem, and they are told that they are to go out and preach the Gospel to the whole world. Most improbable; yet it has come about. Today that Church exists as a world-wide reality.

For a century the Christian Churches have been exposed to venomous hostility, amounting in many cases to violent persecution, such as has not been the fate of any other religious community in the world, with the two exceptions of the Jewish people, and the Baha'i community in Iran. And yet the Churches survive. Divided, worldly, self-seeking, betraying every day the faith which they profess, the Churches still hold on. The *World Christian Encyclopaedia* (1981) tells us, on the basis of a minute survey of the whole of the world, that in this year, 1982, very nearly one-third of all the people in the world call themselves Christians. Christians are more numerous than all the Muslims, Hindus and Buddhists in the world put together. Every Sunday Christ is praised in every part of the world, in far more than a thousand languages. Shamefully unfaithful as the Churches have been, it appears that God still has some part for them to play in his purposes, and that in some way they are still to be instrumental in his hands for the redemption of the world.

Salvation looks to the future. Hinduism and Buddhism do not look forward to a consummation; there is repetition without end, together with a hope of individual deliverance from alienation, from mutability, from the burden of one birth after another almost without end. Islam does look forward to a consummation – to that day of judgment, full of terror for the unbelievers for whom on that day there will be no possibility of escape. The Christian faith, too, is oriented to the future; there will be a day, perhaps in the near future, as the early Christians believed, perhaps in an unimaginably distant age; but whether near or far, that day will be a day of fulfilment, in which all that God has begun to do in Jesus Christ will reach its consummation; time will stop, and only those things that are eternal will remain.

Some streams of Christian tradition have almost excelled the Muslims in their description of the terrors of that day. But this is true neither to the general tone of New Testament teaching nor to the traditions of the early Church. In the museum at Ravenna in Italy there is a large collection of Christian sarcophagi, every single one of which bears the inscription *'Requiescit in pace'*, he sleeps, she sleeps, in peace. This is the true catholic spirit of calm, tranquil expectancy, in the responsible willingness to be ready for him whenever he may call, but also in the sure and certain hope of being called to enter into the joy of the Lord. Somewhere in its history – it is impossible to fix the date with precision – the Church sank into a state of restless nonconformity. *Requiescit,* he sleeps, was changed into *requiescat*, may he rest in peace, confidence changed to anxiety, well-founded trust to uncertainty. It would be well if the catholic confidence could be recovered.

In some of the 'eschatological' passages the hope of salvation, and the very word 'Saviour' appear. 'We await the Saviour from heaven', writes Paul to the Philippians (3:20-21 Gk), 'the Lord Jesus Christ, who will transform this body as we have it now to be conformed to the body of his glory, according to the mighty power through which he is able to subject all things, yes everything, to himself.' 'Vile bodies' says the Authorised Version, and this will not do, even though the word 'vile' is used in its proper Latin sense 'of inferior worth', with no suggestion that the body is either depraved or disgusting. Hinduism does so regard the body – the Tamil classic (*Nāladiyar* 47) writes of this body exuding unpleasantness through all its nine orifices. Some Christian classics yield nothing to the Hindu in contempt and dislike of the body. But this is not Christian. When God created all things, he looked upon all that he made, and saw that it was very good; and this includes the body no less than the spirit of man. The body is beautiful, wonderful in the intricate mechanism of which it is made up, base only because of the unworthy use to which, at times, we submit it. Otherwise how could the Word who came and dwelt among us have been pleased to dwell in a body exactly like ours?

Various better renderings have been suggested. The New English Bible reads 'the body belonging to our humble state', and this is not bad. But I am inclined to think that what it really means is simply 'this physical constitution of our being with all its necessary limitations.' We are tied to these three dimensions of space, time and matter. We are not completely submerged in them, as apparently the animals are. By memory and imagination we can hold past and future before our minds. We can project ourselves in thought from where we are to other and remembered scenes. When our body is behaving itself, we are hardly conscious of it; our hearts go on patiently beating day in day out; we breathe and fill our lungs and are hardly conscious of doing so. For all that, I am tied to this material body with all its susceptibility to injury and sickness, and I can never have another. I am where I am, and can be nowhere else. I am in the present moment, and am writing these lines in Connecticut at 2.25 p.m. (Eastern Standard Time of the USA) on Saturday 17 April 1982. And that is that.

'The body of his glory' seems to mean that existence in which Jesus now is, free from all the limitations which he accepted as the conditions of his visible self-revelation to the human race. As the disciples discovered in the days after the resurrection, where two or three were gathered together in his name he did not so much come as show that he was already there with them. This has been the experience of worshipping groups from that day to this. His presence is not something that is subject to the influence of time and space. Not only so; he shows himself differently and individually to every single believer – Jesus Christ the same yesterday and today and for ever, and yet my experience of him cannot be the same as yours – groom for each bride, and glorified in the range and variety of the experiences that we have of him. This is the body of his glory.

And this is what is meant by the puzzling phrase 'the resurrection of the body'. I shall be I and you will be you to all eternity, but we shall be changed. We can conceive the idea of an existence which is not subject to space or time or matter, but we cannot imagine it; we cannot put precise content into our concept. But this is only to state in other words that, as long as we are here, we have to accept the limitations of our human existence. That, however, is not the end. Christ calls us onward to that of which we now have only dim and uncertain anticipations. He calls us to discover what it means to be truly human, to be redeemed. He gives us, by anticipation, the glorious liberty of the children of God. He invites us to the full and joyful discovery of what it means to be emancipated and to be able to serve with the full uninhibited extent of our being the God whom in Jesus Christ we have come to know and in our sadly dim and imperfect fashion to love.

So we have come to the end of our journey, and we find that all roads lead to Jesus of Nazareth.

In the mysterious story of the transfiguration, we read that the disciples who were with Jesus on the mountain saw also Moses and Elijah talking with him – Moses, the great lawgiver, who spoke with God as a man speaks with his friend; Elijah, the first and in some ways the greatest of the prophets, who when the time came was caught up to heaven and was seen no more. When the disciples looked up again, they saw no man but Jesus only. The others have shared with him all that they could share; then, their work done, they quit the scene, and leave him alone in his glory.

In this book, we have tried to see and hear something of the good and the great of many traditions. We have admired the courage of Muhammad, as he stood alone through passing years for what he believed. We have been drawn by the tranquil beneficence of the Buddha as he continued through his forty years of ministry. We have watched Moses as he climbs the mountain and enters the darkness where God is. We have listened to the sages of Greece, and found that they had strange foreshadowings of the Christ. We have listened to various writers of the Old Testament, and have seen, in parable and hope and vision, 'Jesus through many eyes'. Each has shown us something that is of great value; but to each in turn we have found ourselves obliged to say, 'You are not he.' Each points to one beyond himself, in whom the best that he has to offer is transcended, fulfilled, perfected.

The frightened women at the tomb on the morning of the resurrection are charged with a message – 'Go tell his disciples that he goes before you into Galilee, as he said.' Jesus always goes before us – we never quite catch up with him. Not one of the evangelists has given us the complete picture; we are grateful that we have four of them, and together they help us to know him better. Not one of us can ever know him completely; but we do find that, as we touch the hem of his garment, however blindly and uncertainly, we are touching life. And we have the promise and the assurance that we shall be able to comprehend, *with all the saints,* the breadth and length and depth and height, and to know the love of Christ that passes knowledge (Eph. 3:18-19).

Could we possibly ask for more than this?

If Christ, as thou affirmest, be of men
Mere man, the first and best but nothing more –

Account him, for reward of what He was
Now and for ever, wretchedest of all.
For see; himself conceived of life as love,
Conceived of love as what must enter in,
Fill up, make one with His each soul He loved.

See if, for every finger of thy hands,
There be not found, that day the world shall end,
Hundreds of souls, each holding by Christ's word
That He will grow incorporate with all,
Groom for each bride. Can a mere man do this?
Yet Christ saith, this He lived and died to do.
Call Christ, then, the illimitable God,
Or lost!

Robert Browning, 'A Death in the Desert.'

Index

NORMAN ANDERSON

THE TEACHING OF JESUS

The second book in the new Jesus Library. **Foreword by Michael Green.**

The teaching of Jesus stands on an Everest alone. No other teaching has had the same impact and influence, in countless lives, in diverse cultures and ages. No other teaching has provoked so much change, or stirred so much debate.

Sir Norman presents Jesus' teaching around the central theme of the Kingdom of God. After an introductory chapter on the authenticity of the Gospels, the book falls into three sections: *the summons to the Kingdom,* including the invitation to 'salvation' and 'eternal life'; *the ethics of the Kingdom*, for the individual, the Church and society; and finally *the consummation of the Kingdom,* including the Holy Spirit, the mission of the Church, and the Second Coming.

PROFESSOR SIR NORMAN ANDERSON OBE was Director of the Institute of Advanced Legal Studies in London. He lives in Cambridge and is the author of *The Mystery of the Incarnation.*

F. F. BRUCE

THE HARD SAYINGS OF JESUS

The first volume in the Jesus Library. **Foreword by Michael Green.**

There are two kinds of hard sayings in the Gospels, according to F. F. Bruce: those that are difficult to understand; and those that are easy to comprehend, but all too difficult to put into practice. Seventy of these sayings are explored in detail in this magnificent study.

'Dr F. F. Bruce, one of the most distinguished British New Testament scholars, has set the tone to which other writers in the series will aspire. His book is characterised by clarity, honesty, scholarship, intelligibility, and faith. I know of no book like this, and I am confident that it will reach a very wide circle of readers. The considered fruits of his research and reflection will afford both understanding and confidence to many, and will bring the person of Jesus into clearer focus for every reader.'
Michael Green

DR F. F. BRUCE, formerly Rylands Professor of Biblical Criticism and Exegesis at Manchester University, has recently retired.